TIERRA DULCE

TIERRA DULCE
Reminiscences from the Jesse Nusbaum Papers

By Rosemary Nusbaum

THE
SUN
STONE
PRESS

FIRST EDITION

Book Design: Mina Yamashita

Library of Congress Cataloging in Publication Data:

Nusbaum, Jesse Logan.
    Tierra dulce.

    Bibliography: p. 93.
    Includes index.
    1. Nusbaum, Jesse Logan. 2. Archaeologists--New Mexico--Santa Fe--
Biography. 3. Americanists--New Mexico--Santa Fe--Biography.
4. Santa Fe, N.M.--Biography. 5. Santa Fe--History--Miscellanea.
I. Nusbaum, Rosemary, 1907-   II. Title.
F804.S253N876   978.9'56   80-18365
ISBN 0-913270-83-0

Published in 1980 by The Sunstone Press
                Post Office Box 2321
                Santa Fe, New Mexico 87501

PROLOGUE

To have watched Jesse Nusbaum, a tall ruggedly handsome man,
with a shock of silvery hair and easy gait, walk into a lecture hall
buzzing with people, and to have witnessed the quick hush that
followed, often to hear a whispered, "here comes Jesse,"
was to sense a man of more than ordinary charisma. One sensed
a friend and an expectation that he had something to say to you
that you wanted to hear. His steely blue eyes and his cultured and
unusually deep baritone voice always held an audience.

I could never get him to talk on his own into a tape recorder.
However, if I led with a few questions, he would launch into
the fantastic knowledge he possessed.

If I gained small wisdom in the process and became a humble
narrator, it was because he was a great educator.

   I listened.

                              Rosemary Nusbaum

ACKNOWLEDGEMENT

To Jesse...

Student Maximum — who patiently recorded with me some of the history and stories of his many scientific works and of his many friends... Dedicated to the sciences, but by no means a stodgy individual... A keen sense of humor and a prankster of the first order who found fun along the way.

I saw him a scholar of inspired interests, a proud man with a gift of humility and compassion. As a "Museum man" he lived in the tradition of civility. His sense of dignity and achievement in the preservation of the nation's antiquities are his legacy to America.

Always a teacher, with feet firmly planted on *terra firma* and loving the *tierra dulce*, he believed with me that great instructors of history many times find it helpful to weave a word picture of the time of which they speak...that in man's life, dreams always precede deeds, and with Goethe who said:

> *Our desires are presentiments of the*
> *faculties latent within us and signs of*
> *what we may be capable of doing... we*
> *crave for what we already secretly*
> *possess. Passionate anticipation thus*
> *changes that which is materially*
> *possible into dreamed reality.*

CONTENTS

Part I: THE EARLY YEARS

Part II: THE DEEPER SONG

Part III: THE ANCIENT CITY

Part IV: THE OLD TIME

Part I: THE EARLY YEARS
The Early Years

I was born in Greeley, Colorado, September 3, 1887. The first child of Edward Moore and Agnes Strickland Nusbaum. My mother with her father and the whole family were members of the original Union Colony, which was organized by Horace Greeley and later named after him. The Colony itself was approximately 50 miles north of Denver, an area ten miles square. My grandfather, Alexander Dunbar Moodie, was the first fence rider and each day he rode over it, as they had fenced it.

My father, who journeyed from Salem, Ohio via Kansas City, joined the Colony within a year or so of its founding. He had been apprenticed as a brickmason and he began building in Greeley as soon as he arrived. Within a year or two, father and mother married, and I was the first of four children born to them.

I went to grade school and high school there, and then to Colorado State Normal, where I achieved a Bachelor of Pedagogy in 1907.

During my youth, I was always active, always working. I was apprenticed to my father on the job, backing him up by laying brick and doing other contractural work. He had a reputation for being one of the most competent and honest of men, so there was always plenty of work to do. I got to the point where I could hold up a corner on the laying of pressed brick; I held the line and set the pace. My wages were a dollar extra per day and the going rate was $5 per day for eight hours. I liked edging the bricks in our old "Pug Mill" yard, which sat on the outskirts of town; this was where my father produced most of the bricks that built up the early town of Greeley.

In summertime, in order to earn extra money, I learned photography. My first camera was an old 4x5 Vive that stood vertically and after you took a photo, you pulled a little plug and it dropped. You would think the plate was broken but it wasn't. Next I got a 5x7 view camera and did all of the photographic work for Colorado State Normal School.

I used to spend time collecting agates on the Platte and Cache la Poudre Rivers, where I picked up arrow-points and thus became interested in archaeology. I often went to the home of our family doctor, George Law, to read a book he kept on the lower shelf of a little table which had four brass feet of eagle claws with a glass ball in each one. For fear that I might break the back of the book I always opened it on the floor and lay on my belly to turn the pages. It was the famous monograph of G. Nordenskiöld, *Antiquities of the Mesa Verde*. And thus I got my first great love for the Mesa Verde country.

I specialized at Colorado State Normal in manual arts and science. Upon graduating in 1907, Dr. Snyder recommended me for a position as Professor of Science and the Manual Arts on the faculty of the Las Vegas Normal School at Las Vegas, New Mexico.

After an initial briefing on what was expected of me, I began service under President W.E. Garrison. There was no equipment at all for the manual arts course and it was up to me to get funds for supplies. Mr. Charles Ilfeld of Ilfeld Company in Las Vegas was President of the board and was very receptive, approving everything I needed to start my course. The same followed for the chemistry course, and my students ranged from grades seven through twelve.

Dr. Garrison was especially anxious to develop an interest in athletics. I had played center on the basketball team at Greeley high school, so this activity was natural for me and I started a team, using the Y.M.C.A. gymnasium, as we lacked one of our own. Soon we were playing area schools and winning most of the games.

But I wanted to get back to the things I had enjoyed at Greeley so I bought a motorcycle, a four horse powered belt-driven *Excelsior* and had it shipped to me express. Now I had the freedom to roam the back country over trails, north and west into the mountains and canyons around El Porvenir, into the plains and way to the east and south. The motorcycle took me fishing, hunting clear to Fort Union, up north to Watrus in the days when a large part of the fort was still standing. I was pleased in time to find students who shared an interest in geology and physical geography. It was not long after beginning the course in manual arts when we had an exhibit in the largest furniture store of the town where my students exhibited the pieces they had made for the home: chairs, tables, bookcases and other items all made quite a hit.

Some months passed and one day Dr. Garrison invited me into his office. In a very serious manner he said, "We are perfectly delighted with the way you have taken hold down here; never before have we had so much esprit de corps among the student body. Never before has any person worked as well with the whole student group as you have, but there is one serious thing I want to discuss with you. I doubt that you are 21 years of age, and under New Mexico law, I find we cannot hire a professor who is under 21. I do not want anything to happen as I want you to stay. By the way how old are you?"

"Just 20," I replied.

He shook his head. "I thought you were younger. Couldn't you raise a mustache?"

"Yes, I have at times when off on trips in summertime."

"Can you act a little older?"

I replied that maybe I could, to which he added: "There is one thing I want particularly to caution you about: recently at assembly of the faculty each morning, when you sit on stage, I have noted and the students have noted, with

10

a good deal of mirth I might add, that you were wearing socks that had hearts, spades, diamonds and clubs* — can't you just wear plain socks?"

I said I would wear plain ones.

Everything went fine with him after that; I have never worked with a person who was more cooperative. I was asked to return a second year and I did. Again, they raised my salary offering for a third year, but after two rewarding years in education, I decided my greater interest was in archaeology. I had been given an opportunity to come to Santa Fe to work with Edgar L. Hewett, newly appointed first Director for the Museum of New Mexico, in the old Palace of the Governors in Santa Fe in June 1909.

---

*These were in vogue at the time.

A Mirror for the School

Following the two weeks of lectures in Santa Fe, with short field excursions for the study of antiquities in and around the city, Earl Morris (Earl Halstead Morris, Archaeologist) and I were assigned the task of transporting camping equipment and bedrolls for all the students who were coming out to the El Rito de los Frijoles summer camp for 1911 and the School of American Research under Edgar L. Hewett.

Unable to go by train all the way, we found a small rack-team which we had to push to keep the wheels from being damaged as we went over the deeply rutted old trail from Santa Fe. The horses were pulling a heavy load, and the not heavily travelled horse trail bore to the northwest all the way to Buckman (named for the lumberman Henry S. Buckman), and thence over the Rio Grande which we crossed on the D & RG "chili line" track. From here the little train continued along the west bank of the river, passing first the primitive small station at Otowi, later to become Edith Warner's little "Tea Shop," and then on toward Taos Junction.

Earl and I continued northwest from this lower end to get away from the river, climbing all the way. We knew that the students were due early the next day, and when we finally made it to our destination, it was well after dark. It was 500 feet down into the Rito de los Frijoles Canyon floor and we devised a plan to let down all of our equipment by carrying two suitcases at a time to the cliff edge, padding them with bedrolls, tying a heavy rope around them and dropping them down onto a platform of debris I had made while excavating the previous summer. I told Earl we'd never get all the material down to the very bottom of the canyon, but since there was moonlight, we might chance throwing the lighter objects to the platform, which was about 275 feet below us.

All went well until we came to a large bag, which when we eased it over, struck like a sparkler in the full moon when it landed, making a crashing sound. Startled, we went down to discover a fairly large mirror had been wrapped in the bag. Its owner proved to be a Miss Maud Woy from a girls' school in Denver, and we also found she had a metal dish, short bread cookies from England and other snacks stored away. After this incident, we decided to wait until early the next morning and enlist the help of a few Indians to finish.

The following day after the arrival of the students, I saw Miss Woy speaking to Hewett who called to me and said, "Jess, Miss Woy's mirror and cookies and tea and anchovies which she expected to serve to her friends were ruined last night!"

He held a little wadded-up metal thing, "This was a chafing dish until last night, he said.

I told him straight-faced "Every piece was handled in the same manner and we have had no complaints."

Some years later I ran into Miss Woy's brother who practiced law up in Telluride, and I told him this story. He damned near died laughing.

EL RITO DE LOS FRIJOLES

Today I sat in reverie
Ancient pot-sherds at my feet
Overhead the smudge of Cliff-Dweller's fires
Anasazi made, now eons dead.

The sky shone brilliant, aqua clear
Fat clouds passed in strange fantasy
I wondered? What would the ancients say
Of the trembling harmonies in the world today?

Fine, great pines swayed in a firm brisk breeze
Still here these long years through
Spared by the furies, exile free
Mocking echoes, To mortality.

The little Rio far below
Ran swift and cold and clear
Its same sweet song goes on and on
All harmony with nature's symmetry.

And here a field barren and forlorn
Where once was planted corn
Now only parched wild grasses grow—
Its gift to life, all to the furrow spent.

Why did they leave? How cruel the fate?
This Nation lost in mystery
Only under stern-browed cliffs I see—
Revealed cryptic, symbolic petroglyphs.

Their enemy came not from the skies
Nor yet from 'cross the Seas
But Nomads from the plains...not far
Just 'oer these cloud-capped Jémez peaks.

What pattern then this way of things
I asked the ghosts of Cliff-Dwellers here?
From blackened walls, the skies, the pines—
The Rio clear. A quiet answer...Dwelling Place.

Rosemary Nusbaum

The D & R G and the Red Light

I did a lot of riding on the narrow gauge 'Chili Line,' called that because it went through the best chili growing country in New Mexico. People often rode the line just to buy chili on the train. It ran from Santa Fe on an all day trip to Alamosa, Colorado. The train had one engine, usually one baggage mail car and one or two passenger cars.

Whenever I had to go out of Santa Fe on assignment — photography, archaeology, excavation or setting up camps, I used the little train to ride from town as far as Buckman, at which point I had to climb 1,000 feet to get to the rim of the Pajarito Plateau, then south of that to get to Bandelier National Monument; or if I were due at Puye (which means "where the cottontails meet), I would go up to Espanola, or get off below and walk up from there, or take a cut off across country.

No food was served on the train. It stopped at Embudo a half way point, where you could get lunch. Espanola was not much bigger than Embudo, but it was where Bond and Nohls shipped out cattle, hides, chili, apples and other produce. Bond, a merchant and land owner, owned the large store on the west side of the Rio Grande; there was nothing on the east side. He owned the Baca land which was the great Valle Grande area. Valle Grande is the site of the largest extinct volcanic crater in the world and cattle and some sheep were grazed there in summer. The stock was driven to Buckman before winter for drives to Santa Fe or to the North and the little train transported them in small numbers only.

The train ran every day but Sunday. The first time I rode it out of Santa Fe the fellow from the mail car came over to me and introduced himself as Mr. A. Wood, then when we were well on our way he returned to ask me if I would like to do some reading. When I said yes, he reached into a bag he carried over his shoulder and handed me a half dozen tracts titled "Come to Jesus."

About four trips later I learned there had been an operational upset on the railroad because Wood had begun to push his religious bent more vigorously and had done away with the U.S. Railway cancelling stamps, replacing it with one of his own that said "Come to Jesus" and showing a flag.

When the Wood stamp came out, people began kicking about it, with result that an inspector showed up and Wood was told that if he ever used that stamp again, charges of insubordination would be filed against him. Well, it about broke his heart and people claimed that as he stamped the mail thereafter, he would loudly recite, "Come to Jesus! Come to Jesus!"

At this time Wood was married to Donazetta (Museum of New Mexico Assistant Librarian and then Librarian 1910-1911. She later became Mrs. Edgar L. Hewett.) They lived in the little red brick house on the corner of Don Gaspar and Manhattan. Wood was in the habit of taking men from the Penitentiary

14

south of town to "Christianize" them. He clothed and fed them in so many numbers that Donazetta divorced him.

After Embudo the train had to climb rather sharply to get to the top of the grade where passengers and mail and other commerce for Taos got off at Taos Junction. As the train came in from Buckman, which is a long climb to the top of the Divide on a long trestle, you could look down toward the US. Indian School, north and west of town and see over Santa Fe.

The first time I came in I had been talking to the brakeman and conductor when the whistle sounded. I looked over and showing through the trees were three red lights. One was flashing on and off about a quarter mile away.

"What's that light?" I asked.

"Oh, that's the way they greet us down there," the conductor said. "We have to take the train up to the station, then we have to back down and turn it around to get it ready to go the next day. We always take a little walk over to a house down there where they have good beer and dancing, plus a good deal of sporting. They always signal us that way. The bar is run by the wife of the sheriff."

A Day with the Penitentes

Each year as Easter approaches the people of New Mexico and Southern Colorado manifest a growing interest in the rites of the Hermanos Penitentes. I would like to tell you an interesting experience I had with them, Rosemary.

Throughout the two years I spent teaching at Las Vegas, there was much local curiosity about the Penitentes who were then active and strong in New Mexico. They are followers of a flagellant and fanatical religious order which was active in various parts of Europe about the 13th century and survived in remote districts as late as the 16th. Popular opinion ascribes their appearance on this Continent to a few Spaniards who brought their rites with them.

Because they practice the doctrine of flagellation in atonement of their sins of the past year, their almost pagan rites are wholly confined to the week preceding Easter, known to us as Holy Week but often termed Penitente week in New Mexico. Their activities increase in severity until the climax is reached on Good Friday. At all other times they are but little different from other Christians.

I had my motorcycle and had become familiar with some of the villages and I had spotted a number of their Moradas. Among my friends on the faculty was a native born Mexican American who had grown up in a small village with the Penitentes and was considered an authority on their ceremonies.

On Good Friday of 1908, the two of us set out very early on my motorcycle for a day of participation and sight-seeing starting for Mora, 33 miles to the North. About three miles above Sapello, I knew where a Morada sat in a canyon, but found no activity there so we pushed on. We had gone about three more miles when we came upon a procession of five. We passed them and then stopped noticing their looks were about as wicked as I've ever seen. I remembered the warnings of the people of Las Vegas who had said they were the most treacherous of the natives. We decided to pull out while we had the chance and nothing could be gained by waiting.

From here the rocky and muddy dirt road went over rather high mountains. Finally we arrived at the top of a high divide to find stretched below the most beautiful mountain valley imaginable. Rociada, Gascón and Peñasco Blanco all Penitente settlements are located in this valley, but as our chances at Mora were better we continued on until we passed the foot of the New Mexican village of Peñasco Blanco, where a crowd of about 100 people were gathered in the field several hundred yards below a Morada. Again it seemed as inaccessible a place as possible at the three large crosses of Calvary standing on a slight hill.

We must have been about a quarter of a mile from them. Guards were located on all points from which anything of the ceremony could be seen and would have moved us on. We had a clear view through our field glasses and watched the crowd at the crosses as well as the eight members who were tortur-

16

ing themselves in front of the Morada. Their bloody backs were clearly visible and we counted about 15 crosses set in the ground at intervals leading from the Morada to the small knoll or El Calvario—Calvary where three crosses stood and where the crowd was assembled.

We could clearly see the body of a human or image tied to the center cross, but while I was sure it was a human, my companion said that it was only a life-sized image of the Savior as he had witnessed this as a child. He said they used to crucify one of their members each Good Friday, one who had divulged the secrets of the sect being the first choice; then if none were traitors they asked for volunteers and if none volunteered, one was chosen by lot to be crucified.

Years ago they were nailed to the cross, but strict territorial laws plus excommunication of the Penitentes by the Catholic Church have put an end to crucifixions. They are now back in the good graces of the Church but in some remote areas such as this the penitent is bound to the middle cross by thongs, so tightly that they would cut into the flesh and cause the blood to stop circulating. This cross was raised by the members and set in the soft dirt and left until the penitent lost consciousness before he was taken down and into the Morada to be revived, which usually takes several hours and in cases he has been known to die without regaining consciousness. All the time he is on the cross the people stand quietly below waiting for the time when life is supposed to be extinguished.

A crown of native cactus-thorns is usually worn on the head at this time and the face and whole head are masked. I could not say whether what we were watching from that distance was a real crucifixion or not, but no movements were noted. I will always be inclined to think the penitent was unconscious. We were waiting to see the body taken down when we were spotted by the guards and we quickly moved on for they followed us for some distance and waited there.

We continued on to another divide and soon were once again in a beautiful valley: high mountains on three sides covered with heavy timber and on the west the snowy range of the Rockies. Mora is the county seat of Mora County in northern New Mexico and it's a typical town of about 600 people, mostly of Spanish extraction and a few dozen anglos. All the buildings are of adobe with the exception of a few of stone, which left a feeling of being foreign.

The natives who were not Penitentes flocked about my motorcycle, the first one seen in that part and a great curiosity. From their manner I saw they would quickly have loosened every bolt and detachable thing. Fortunately we learned that there was great Penitente activity in the area of Cleveland, a small community above Mora and we left at once. We had not gone many miles when we spotted a fine procession through our glasses. They were led by the Hermano Mayor, the chief officer of this lodge and followed by four Rezadors, or prayer chanters whose sounds, especially in the night, sound more like the howl of coyotes than anything I've ever heard. My native companion explained that their role was to follow the near-naked Penitentes, each of whom we could see bearing a hugh cross cut from green timber at least 12 feet long and weighing in most cases about 200 pounds or more; in many cases so heavy that the penitent has to rest the arm on the ground every rod or so and has to accept an assist from a compañero to again raise it to his shoulder. The long end drags on the ground and not infrequently the compañero will help him carry it.

We saw that the bearers of the crosses were followed by the usual pitaros or flute players and after these, we could see those that followed scourging themselves. Those doing penance were clad only in a pair of white muslin knee-length drawers and their heads were covered. My companion informed me that on an occasion like this he had witnessed them walking barefoot over rocks, cacti, etc., for long distances, and over rough mountain trails to the cross of Calvary where exercises were held before the return to the Morada, always kneeling before the cross directly in front of the Morada door before entering it again.

A good part of the ceremony takes place in the Morada. The picador is the man who does the first torturing and he begins by cutting three ugly gashes in the back with a sharp knife of flint called a pedernal, then he pricks the back with sharp pieces of glass. This is called the work of atonement. Next he takes a heavy knotted scourge, which I would say is not unlike a plant root, for I have seen them — quite harmless until filled with blood and hardens with the lashings. The Penitent asks for "three meditations of the Passion of Our Lord" and is given six strokes with all the strength of the strong Picador, three on each side of the back. The Penitent then asks for and receives "five wounds of Christ," then "the seven last words," and the "forty days in the wilderness." As each demand calls for a stroke on each side of the back, that makes in all about 130, which is severe as the scourge cuts deeper with each stroke.

In some remote areas, cacti are bound to the body and heavy bundles must be carried on the bare back. The longer the Penitent can stand up to these punishments the more esteemed he is among the others. At Rociada a party of Las Vegas people passed a procession of the Penitentes who had cacti and bailing wire wound into their scourges so that each cut might be more painful and draw blood. The crown of thorns is worked about so that the thorns penetrate the scalp.

We had learned at Mora that the night before over 20 of the Los Hermanos de Noche had carried wooden crosses over a high mountain to the Morada at Cebolla, a distance of over four and a half miles and back again. We decided to leave to follow the trail of the crosses up this hill and noting where the free ends of the crosses had dragged we could tell by the packed condition of the ground just where stops had been made. It was no small task to push my motorcycle up the hill that would have taken four horses to pull a Mexican wagon to its top.

At night lanterns are used to find the way and generally a gigantic metraca sounds continuously — its an instrument like a rattle made of a ribbed piece of wood within which a limber piece mounted in a frame rotates. It makes an incessant noise which resembles in a way the sounds made by the smaller metracas used during street carnivals in Mexico. Seeing a procession like this at night, marching through the mountain fastness, with lanterns swinging, the crunching of the heavy crosses on rocky ground, the weird chanting of the rezadors combined with the shrill tones of the carito flute and fife can fill the strongest of humans with sheer horror and haunt one with its lasting impression.

At Cebolla, located at the foot of the Morada on the mountainside, we came into a large group. It seemed the entire town must be assembled and with some timidity we stopped the motorcycle as one of the men approached. We were surprised to find he used some English and seemed curious about the motorcycle and finally he responded by telling us "it's a day of prayer and song." We asked if we might join in and he left to ask the others. All were now looking our way and a group of the men came over to say they had never seen a motorcycle at close range before and several asked rides and asked my companion to explain the mechanism to them. This he tried to do and the one who spoke some English in turn explained to them. I obliged a number of them and we shared oranges and other edibles we had with us. In turn they became quite cordial and we were invited to the women's church where a Penitente was praying to the women who all remained for a long period on their knees on the hard earth. They had an altar set up at one end of this empty hut: A simple crude table with a colorful wallpaper stretched behind it and in front and hanging from this were a number of crucifixes.

All the older women were dressed in black. Rebozos covered their heads and only their eyes and noses were visible. The youngest girls all wore their hair down covering their backs and each one wore a royal purple ribbon about one inch in diameter around her head and across her forehead. In each case the hair was center-parted. The girls of marriageable age, between 14 and 18 and usually an average of less than 15, wore yellow and green dresses. We were being watched very closely in the church and had been warned not to use a camera. Our 4 x 5 was hidden in our lunch sack but we kept the faith and toward dusk were told we might wait until the procession of hermanos returned.

We waited and watched as did the others staying well in the background and not feeling very comfortable. Dusk had settled when long before they came into sight we could hear the wailing notes of the fifes and flutes and always that blood-curdling eerie chant. They were coming very slowly toward the Morada. Now and then as a compañero passed with his lighted lantern we caught a glimpse of one of the Penitentes stooped over by the weight of the immense cross. We could see only one man stripped and still trying to scourge himself but that was enough. He was supported by two compañeros and so weak from loss of blood and the ten mile trip over the rough, rock mountain trail, that tho he was still holding the scourge with both hands and occasionally able to strike a blow over his head to reach his already bloody, bare back, he would fall to the earth when the guards let go and had to be dragged for short distances. As he drew nearer we could see the mask over his head was bloody as were his drawers clotted with blood in the cold. His back was one raw sore. His feet were bloody.

Most behind him were walking the 'penance step." It is a slow walking gait with the body bent far over as tho setting out cabbages or other plants. They are not permitted to straighten up so torture is increased. A hard wind began to blow. We shivered at that altitude probably not under 8,000 feet and our uneasiness began to grow, as tho we were intruders on a sight not meant for us. The hour was nine and night well settled upon us when we quietly turned and pushing our motorcycle some distance before daring to start the motor, headed back to Las Vegas.

The Penitentes are dying out around here these days, Rosemary, and their rituals belong to the past. But you witnessed an incident in Alcalde just a few years ago that must have been Penitentes: There were three native men struggling under the weight of crosses like those I saw. The men wore flowing, biblical-like white cotton garments and their shoulders were heavily stained with bright red blood. They laboriously pulled these crosses to the front of the Catholic church there, laid them down with help, knelt briefly in front of the Church and then went in for about 15 minutes. Once again struggling under their heavy burden, which could not have been lifted, but dragged to a permanent large cross set in a nearby field. The cross was a familiar sight to Taos-bound travelers, but is no longer there now. When the men reached this cross the Penitentes put down their burdens and prostrated themselves before the large cross. That was the entire ceremony — for you said you heard no chanting and there was no accompaniment of sounds of anykind.

Edgar L. Hewett

Edgar L. Hewett was difficult in the earlier days...always taking leads where he thought he'd get a following. He wanted things done fast, you'd do it and then he would leave for the Near East, Athens or Rome and then casually take credit for your work. He had studied law, just enough to threaten suits if he did not get his own way. As he grew older he became more fearful of change and improvement. He fought the ideas of younger men.

Kidder (Alfred V. Kidder, archaeologist) at the Pecos Ruins had a hard time. Ideas other than his own were an anathema to Hewett and he opposed them. Or take the time Dr. Corwin (R.W. Corwin, M.D.) came here from Minnequa Hospital in Pueblo, Colorado, with John D. Rockefeller, Jr. who wanted to do something for Corwin because he had been on the Board of the School of American Research since its inception: After a trip to Rito de los Frijoles, Rockefeller went to Hewett and told him he would like to assist him in some way by doing something for the school. He proposed for consideration the possibilities that (1) the Palace of the Governors be made an historic project, for it not to have pottery exhibits throughout as this seemed incorrect; (2) art should be a separate building; and (3) there should be one for archaeology and one for ethnology, to study the living Indians, their ways and culture.

He told Hewett, "I understand you have a very fine little City library, also a Supreme Court library. I know from past experience that one unified library, under proper management results in better service. Space for all this could be taken clear up to Marcy Ave. Try to get this property." Hewett thanked him saying it was a nice idea and would consider it. He did, but feared that the use of Rockefeller's money would dictate policy and subtly he opposed it.

Mr. Rockefeller made a second visit with his wife and found Hewett had stacked all the pottery down in the basement of the Art Museum after it had been built. Mr. Rockefeller asked me to arrange for them to see some pottery making at the Pueblos. I told him I was not free to leave Mesa Verde at that time, but advised him to call K.M. Chapman, "announce yourself and then hold the phone." Later I learned that Chap had said he was on part time and could arrange the trip on his own time with pleasure. He did; Hewett heard of it, called Chap and remonstrated him, "Chap, you stay here, this whole plan is mine. I am responsible for everything."

I had been working on a tentative plan along the line of Mr. Rockefeller's thinking with Kidder, Wissler (Clark Wissler: Officer with the Museum of Natural History in New York) and others and now Mr. Rockefeller asked Chap to work up a plan for him. Chap at once began looking into the possible acquisition of the proposed property up to Marcy Ave. He succeeded in securing options on the whole block clear to Marcy for the sum of $140 thousand, and

Hewett bluntly refused to consider it.

After hearing this Hewett presented his own counterplan. It involved work in Asia, the Near East, Mongolia, Siberia and all over the U.S. He sent it in, while sending Chap out on a number of irrelevant assignments, to keep him out of the way. He then called a meeting back east of the Board of the Archaeological Institute of America and got them to approve his plan. He mailed it, not to Rockefeller direct, but to the Rockefeller Foundation, which is entirely separate. After considering the matter and voting on it they turned it down.

Meanwhile, what had occurred came to Rockefeller's attention whereupon he criticized the Foundation's action saying it was a personal matter. He then sent for me. I went directly to his home at 10 West 54th Street in New York City. In this meeting with me, he assured me, that he was sincere and was desirous that everything be fair and all in agreement.

This is where it really started. He recognized that New Mexico was a small state, but a worthy center for cultural research and was willing to assist in promoting to greater advantage, what had already begun. He was aware that Hewett had refused to cooperate with the options Chap had laid out — that the majority of us had agreed the concentration of effort should be kept in the Southwest with Santa Fe the focal place — and wanted his way alone.

We then agreed that the 57 acre site on Camino Lejo and Old Pecos Road offered by the Misses Martha and Elizabeth White and attorney Francis C. Wilson would be the place. This is why the Laboratory of Anthropology was built where it is and not joined up with the Museum. Hewett fought an all out effort against the Laboratory. He fought me the whole time I was its Director, even going to Washington to try to get me fired from my position with the National Park Service, from which I was on leave to the Laboratory. I had to stand up against him for the Laboratory, for it was my responsibility.

He always worked through his "Women's Board" knowing they would influence their husbands. He chose them with great care and he used them the whole time, quoting "my Woman's Board," knowing the majority were on his side and depended on their husbands to convince the people of the community on his behalf. This bit of strategy was generally quite successful. He helped himself to my personal photograph collection, never once giving me credit for one of them.

I wasn't alone in my impressions of Hewett. I recall one night sitting up until the small hours while the empty bottles of Scotch Vat 69 grew interesting. We were at the old Cassidy House on Canyon Road, then being rented to and lived in by the late archaeologist Oliver Ricketson Jr., and listening to hair-raising stories of Revolutions in Mexico and Guatemala.

In attendance that night were Sylvanus G. Morley, J. Eric Thompson and Oliver Ricketson, Jr., all of the Carnegie Institution of Washington. Dwight W.

22

Rife (one of the authors of the 1933 Carnegie Institution publication *The Peninsula of Yucatan*) and Mr. Shufeldt who had been with the P.W. Shufeldt Co. and had helped organize the transport of the 14th Central American Expedition April 5 to May 5 1931 up the Rio Usumacinta to Yaxchilan in the State of Chiapas, Mexico were also there. "Shue" had been a chiclero for the Wrigley Co. and at this time was living in retirement at the Old Mill near Mora, New Mexico.

This night Hewett's name came up distastefully several times regarding his relations with others. Again recently a communication from Thompson in England sent us this little verse composed by Beatrice Blackwood, an English woman with the Pilt-River Museum, Oxford, England, who had been a member of Hewett's archaeological field camp in the Jemez Canyon:

> There was an old duffer called Hewett
> Who was head of the School—and he knew it.
> When anyone came,
> Who knew naught of his fame
> He took out his trumpet, and blew it.

The Duke of Tulum

This adventure really began in the first four months of 1910 when Edgar L. Hewett, Director of the School of American Archaeology at Santa Fe, sent Sylvanus G. Morley, his Mayan research scholar, and me as photographer and assistant to the great ruins at Quiragua, Guatemala (see Morley: *The Inscriptions of Peten.* Vol. I, pp. 85-86). We surveyed and photographed the mounds and courts; set up stelae and removed the dense forest moss and lichens, which had all but obliterated the exceptional sculpturing and epigraphy of these monuments.

Again in January 1913, with the addition of J.P. Adams, graduate engineer and surveyor, Hewett again dispatched us hastily to complete the cleaning of dense jungle from a 20-acre tract to be excavated. This acreage was on United Fruit Company land, who had graciously set aside the land we needed and cleared a fire-break, so that when trees were felled and jungle burned to plant bananas, no damage would be done to our excavation site. It was a whale of a job and was the first effort made to preserve and document these monuments.

This completed, Hewett sent Morley and me to Chichen Itzá and Uxmal, with orders for me to photograph using my 5 x 7 glass negatives, make movies and gain a complete record of the major ruins and of the culture and home life of the Itzá. This was to be used for his notable Mayan culture exhibit at the upcoming Panama Pacific Exposition in San Diego in 1915.

Morley had studied this area and the more he thought about it the more it fascinated him. I was photographing as much as I could. From Chichen Itzá we went to Uxmal and repeated our pattern and from there we went to the walled city of Campeche, the farthest place to the South: beyond was "bad country." Vay was suffering from amoebic dysentery and I was hit by a debilitating malaria. This walled city still served as a fort and strong hold and we found some of the finest examples of early structures still standing. It had been built at the time the hijackers were coming in and erected it for protection. I got some of my finest pictures here for things were rapidly deteriorating and tumbling down.

Vay decided we must go back to Chichen Itzá for more details and it was there we got word from Hewett to proceed "at once" to Tulum, to research and photograph. We knew that the Sublevato Maya, those Itzá who remained unconquered and unchristianized, who lived south of the ruins of Tulum in the territory of Quintana Roo were in an ugly mood. Chichen Itzá is the nearest approach to Tulum across land, but the jungle was impassible for us at this time and we were ordered to proceed by boat.

It was here that I learned from Morley the story of Edgar Thompson and his exploits while serving as U.S. Consul in Yucatán. He had stayed at the same house with Thompson, who was also looking after the entire Chichen Itzá area for the Armour Co., who, through lease, controlled the whole Chichen complex

24

and were raising cattle there. Thompson had become ardently interested in collecting Maya artifacts. At this time so much material of jade and gold was higraded from the great Sacred Cenote at Chichen Itzá. (The peninsula of Yucatán was higher than sea level but because of heavy rainfall part of the year, the soft, fresh rainwater leached down to the general sea level: thus dissolving the roof. Being unsupported, it caved in. Where weaknesses developed the existing savannahs and cenotes occurred.) Alfred M. Tozzer working through the Peabody Museum at Harvard arranged an exhibit of some of it. When it was seen, hell was raised and Teddy Roosevelt had a hand in returning some of it. It was last exhibited at the leading Museum of Mexico City.

Vay knew that Thompson had once been in Tulum going by bush, with some good Mayan friends. He had started to make a mold of a small stela that was there, but had suddenly taken violently ill and lapsed into unconsciousness. His friends had quickly gotten him out of there and his illness turned out to be yellow fever. He recovered and went back to Chichen Itzá. According to Morley's information the little stela had been left, "lightly buried". Morley was most anxious to see this little stela.

We knew further that in their 1842 visit to Tulum, Stephens and Catherwood reported and sketched the finding of this small stela. In 1911, two Englishmen, Howe and Parmalee buried this small stela in the sand when they were forced to flee the second day from hostile Indians. All this took place before the Carnegie Institution of Washington entered the area for research and restoration. It was this stela that Morley was now sure would have the initial series date glyph of such tremendous interest to him.

It was now April and we heard an announcement that the ranking military guard, a General in Yucatán, then in Merida was soon going to sail from the port of Progresso via Cazumel Island, to subjugate the Sublevato Maya Indians. Morley conferred with this general, Guia Luiz at once, expressing high interest in accompanying him and was welcomed. He said his sailing vessel with a crew of ten men and a machine gun would sail from Progresso at 10:30 a.m. the following day. Morley told him he would arrange for the delivery of several cases of beer and that we would arrive early the next day, with food and our impedimienta, photographic and other baggage.

When we arrived at the dock we found out that the General's sloop had departed several hours earlier. Never had I seen Morley so angry. He telegraphed the circumstances to his intimate friend and collaborator, President Huerta in Mexico City. It was Huerta who had established the Military Reservation and the Penal Colony at Santa Cruz de Bravo for controlling the Sublevato Maya from south of Tulum. Huerta promptly wired Morley that he had radioed the captain of the naval gunboat transporting food, supplies and prisoners, to the penal colony to pick us up at Progresso, drop us off at San Miguel in Cazumel,

25

then pick us up a week later enroute back to Progresso.

Our experience on that boat was a horrible one. The habits of the prisoners were the filthiest imaginable. The ones that scrubbed the decks cleaned up by pushing it over the side. The heat and odor were so bad, Morley and I could not stand it below. We got under a landing raft on deck to keep out of their way. We fell into a sleep and were awakened by slop water deliberately being thrown on us. They knew we were U.S. citizens and were very sharp and critical. The Captain and first mate made their distaste very obvious. We were fortunate that Huerta was strong for archaeology, since he had followed Porferio Diaz and Modero, neither of whom were as friendly. Morley was seasick as usual, and I was secretly jubilant when we cast anchor at Cazumel and got off that gunboat. Here we learned that General Guia Luiz had been severely censured by Huerta for leaving us high and dry at Progresso.

At San Miguel, the principal port of the Island of Cazumel, Morley got busy right away and shortly had arranged for a small dory to take us across the narrow neck of the Gulf of Honduras to Tulum about eight leagues (24 miles) to Tulum. A crew was a different matter. The Commandante of the port told us it would be hazardous to attempt to go to Tulum because of the hostility of the Sublevado Itzá and he could not clear us. However he offered clearance to Chacalah, which was on the mainland four leagues south of Tulum. We were only interested in going straight across, so Vay used his old trick and got a crew by distributing $5 gold pieces to each and a $10 one for the Captain.

He used gold, because that is what they wore and prized above any other thing. This was the price we finally paid to get where we wanted to go and keep from landing four leagues, or 12 miles south of Tulum. We finally lined up a crew of nine. Four natives for boatmen and five armed with single barreled shotguns for bodyguards.

As was our poor luck the Gulf was stormy and all hands got drunk on the first night out.

They drank white eye — straight alcohol. They always have it down there. We were all night on that dory and sighted our destination at 8:30 the next morning. Passing three smaller ruins, on the low lying bluff and on the highest part, which is very rough, irregular and undercut were the plainly visible terraced rear walls of the Castillo.

We found a place where the surf wasn't so bad and old limestone had caved off and there were reefs. Our boat was about 200 yards out. We couldn't get any nearer and left men on the dory to care for it. Finding ourselves about a half a mile south of the ruin, we cast anchor. When all was ready our small periagua or dug out, cast off with five of us, laden with cameras, guns, machetes, lunch and fresh water, making for a small sandy beach. No sooner had we cast off than our periagua began to fill with water from the heavy sea, notwithstanding our desperate efforts to "bail it out." The natives used every language at their disposal to express their feelings and we had to depend on a particularly efficient knowledge of Spanish and English to urge them on. Morley had his own brand of mingling Spanish and English and I have never heard this "Morleyana" used more effectively.

We managed to ride the first roll of the surf but the second overturned us, spewing us out into the sea. The next 15 minutes were spent fishing out equipment and getting ashore. I got through with three dry plate-holders for the camera. Our condition was now pathetic. Photographic equipment waterlogged. After this I had to use just the cap because the shutter wouldn't work at all. The guns were full of water and sand. They were muzzle loaders and the first thing the drunken crew did was to pull the triggers to try to fire the guns. But they couldn't get the powder charge out.

The heavy sea would not permit us to return to the dory. We were within a half a mile of the main shrine and the outpost of Tulum Maya and we were defenseless should we be seen or encounter any hostility. After looking for some time at the angry sea we decided to take our chances with the Indians.

We proceeded slowly along the rocky bluff cutting our way through a very dense growth of scrub palms and thorny bushes, until we reached an outer wall of Tulum ruins. This gigantic wall of masonry, enclosing a rectangular space with two arms extending, was some 600 feet back from the sea and was connected by a 1500 foot section at the rear extremities which enclosed the main group of ruins.

Narrow arcades open through the north and south sections of the wall and one, about midway, opens through the long western section. The arcade through which we passed is 26 feet long and about 15 feet high, is laid up roughly with out the use of mortar and narrows down to about 20 feet in thickness on either side of the arches.

Large watchtowers surmount the walls at the corners. Within the large and enclosed rectangle, the jungle was so thick that one had to hack his way wherever he went, except near the main castillo where the natives, who made constant excursions to the temple on top of the pyramid, had cut away all vegetation. To move through this jungle is hard work at best, and it was doubly hard for us since we expected to be attacked by savage Indians any minute.

'From the time we left Cazumel, Morley munched on his box of crackers to deter the taste of bile. I took a picture of him in a bad spell in the early morning light, sleeping on a little bit of a bench in utter misery. I have seen him oblivious to babies crying, chickens cackling in cages right next to him on any deck. He would become famished and dehydrated and just the sight of a body of water sickened him. So it was in Tulum that day.

The castillo with its two lower level wings is about 100 feet long. The main temple is set flush with a nearly perpendicular sea wall of block shape structure and leaves a small platform in front and to the side. A grand stairway 30 feet wide with low balustrades still intact, ascends the front portion of the structure to the temple above.

Entrance is gained by three medium sized rectangular doorways separated by two round stone columns. Within there is a narrow corridor six feet wide, joined by a single doorway to a rear corridor nine feet wide. Low side benches of masonry construction are found on three sides of the inner room and at the ends of the front corridors. Narrow oblong openings give scant light to the rear room, but they command a wondrous view of the sea.

Construction of this temple is typically Mayan. All outside walls are perpendicular while the longer inside walls, at a height of six or seven feet, taper gradually inward until they are within a few inches of touching. A flat capstone is placed over this gap and a foot or more of rough lime mortar forms the roofing material, and this becomes what is commonly known as the Mayan arch.

The outside wall is usually divided into two equal horizontal bands, the lower remaining smooth, plain and undecorated, while the upper carries nearly all the decorative elements. The upper band of this building has the usual offsets. The principal decoration consists of three niches, or depressed panels, placed directly over the doorways, with stucco figures. The center one is well preserved and represents a guard with an elaborate headdress in an inverted position. The other two are more or less mutilated and not well preserved.

At the corners the entablature assumes the form of animal heads in low flat relief. Typical Mayan decorative elements are spread evenly over the inner part of the entablature. On either side of the ground level are larger less ornate buildings with the peculiarity of roofs (now fallen in). Roofs are very rare in Mayan construction and so far as is known, they are only found irregularly as far as Quintana Roo. The rooms are large and in their central axia two columns were erected, to suitable heights, making three equal spaces of these and to the wall. Double Zapote-lintels were laid and crossed transversely by a pair of smaller logs reaching from the center to the side walls. On this latticed framewood the roofing of rock and mortar was laid to a depth of nearly one foot.

Directly in front of the Castillo and above the regularly shaped court are seven other structures. One, very elaborate, has a five door-four column entrance with a sanctuary in the rear room and a second story directly above. Generally when a second story was added, the lower one was filled with rock and mortar to make a stable foundation for the heavy construction overhead.

The interiors of the entrance and portal after being evenly plastered were completely covered with colored murals representing the life of the people. We found them extremely well preserved in part. The cenote or well which supplied the community with fresh water is located near the surrounding wall north of the Castillo. (The above description is, in part, from the Morley/Nusbaum Report in the Denver *Republican*, July 28, 1913.)

Morley had frantically begun searching through the sand for the stela in a spot where he thought the two Englishmen had probably buried it in 1911 when the hostile Tulum Maya were seen approaching. He did not find any part of the initial date for the monument at this time. We remained for several hours about the ruins. It is hardly necessary to state that our presence did not become known to the Indians, else this report would never have been written. The greatest possible precautions were taken to keep our presence a secret.

After taking a final view of the wonderful expanse of jungle visible from the highest point of the Castillo, we returned stealthily to the shore, woke the drunken guards and prepared to return to the dory. We finally reached the dory after a number of upsets in the boiling surf, only to find that the heavy sea had made terrible work of it. It was so badly wrenched, bounding up and down, that bad leaks had developed and we took turns working the crude pumping device continuously to keep up with the leakage. Vay was too seasick to help. When we were well underway the crewmen put out a line and in no time they had caught a barracuda and were cooking it on deck, happily gorging on warm, almost raw fish.

No Broadway hotel ever looked brighter to us, or more inviting than the little thatched-roof cantina where we took our belated evening meal. From there we went to Valladolid — where several people got shot that night. Early the next morning we got out of there and went to Dzitas which was the farthest they would let us go into the territory of Quintana Roo to trade and I got a fine hammock. We proceeded to Uxmal but found much drinking and illness, so we left for Copan, spending a short time there before returning to Santa Fe. J. Eric Thompson (eminent British Mayan scholar, knighted by Queen Elizabeth in 1976), upon hearing this story dubbed me "The Duke of Tulum." Ever since the name has stuck in great good humor.

Rosemary, you had been in Chichen Itzá and Uxmal too, but many years after this experience we were there once again on our honeymoon in 1947. We found it much changed. It has been handsomely restored, but what had been the magnificent hacienda near there, where Morley and I stayed outside of Uxmal, was as you saw, in ruins. The great sunken garden visible still, but had been long neglected and the Chapel had the cross of "the black Christ" still hanging amid the squalor. We were there in '47 partly because Vay had come to you before our marriage and had said: "Daughter, you know that the sword of Damocles (referring to a coronary attack a few months before) hangs over my head and I want you to marry my cherished friend Jess and bring the girls (Rosemary and Lavinia Rife) to be with Frances and me at Chen Ku (the Morley's hacienda out-side Merida)." So it happened we went to Yucatan once again that Christmas to

29

be joined by our good friends, Neil P. Macphail, M.D., Superindendent of the United Fruit Company hospital at Quiragua, who had seen me through a bout of malaria years before, and his sister Jessie and their chief-nurse, Miss Alerby. We have great souvenir memories of that time: the dinner of honor with the Molina family of Merida; midnight Mass with them when the Archbishop paid Vay a small tribute; and a never-to-be-forgotten Christmas dinner when the American Consul arrived to be greeted by our beloved little Lavinia, who, upon seeing a calendar under his arm (it was to be a gift to the family) ran back and answered the query "who is it?" for all to hear, "Oh, never mind Uncle Vanus, it's only a calendar salesman."

The General's Uniform

We were down at the ruins of Quirigua and Edgar Hewett wanted to make sure that all the pictures I had made were good, so I said, "Well I've tried to develop them down here but it's damp, hot and unsatisfactory. I need to get to Guatemala City where the water is cold and fresh and the nights sufficiently cool for photo developing." So we all went up to the Grand Hotel for a two day stay. I spent a good deal of time away from my assigned quarters processing my 5 x 7 glass plates. When I returned to my room I found that a chap named Thompson, auditor for the United Fruit Co. had been assigned to share the room with me. Also, there in the room were two beautiful large sole-leather suitcases I had not seen and I said to him, "Say Thompson, you will pauperize the United Fruit Co buying stuff like this." He replied, "They aren't mine." "Then what the hell are they doing here?" I said. He answered, "I don't know, let's have a look."

In one we found a General's uniform, the other an Admiral's, with a magnificent sword, all chased in gold. I tried on the coat and found it so large I had to stuff two pillows in my chest to button it up; my whiskers were long and it looked interesting. Thompson got into the other but we had to wrap the belt around him twice to keep it from dragging on the ground with the sword. We decided to give it a try and wear them around when Jack Adams came in and he took our picture, in which we tried to look properly important.

Charles Lummis (the historian/writer) was registered there so we went over to his room, tapped on his door with the sword and demanded to be admitted "in the name of the King of Spain." He took a quick look, got excited and said: "You damned fools you; they'll pick up you, have you in their penitentiary and beat you to death. What would you say if a couple of Guatemalan's were to come into the White House, dressed in U.S. Officer's uniforms with Teddy Roosevelt there?" I said, "Well, Teddy would look after 'em."

Lummis was speaking from experience, as he was with the Archaeological Institute of America at this time. He had been librarian for the City of Los Angeles and had published a little magazine called *Sunset*. He had walked great distances across the Southwest and had spent two years at Isleta (Indian Pueblo). This is where the penitentes shot him one night. He had given them wine at San Mateo, a penitente village near the foot of Mt. Taylor, and then taken and published pictures of their penitente ceremonies.

He was shot through the cheek, but a heavy wallet of manuscripts he carried over his heart stopped another bullet. I always thought of him as a western John Muir. He kept his young son Quimu with him a good deal. He was a keen writer, a walking encyclopoedia, most able to express himself, but not a professional archaeologist. He loved to wear white lace-like shirts, with a red undershirt to show the outer lace design. The men of Isleta affected them and with this he wore an embroidered band about his waist.

He counted Teddy Roosevelt among his friends and this day, when he answered the door he was wearing one of several muted-colored corduroy suits he liked and wore even in the tropics. In the right pocket of his jacket were the usual 50 or so cheroots he always carried with these suits. I have watched him many times ceremoniously light one by removing a piece of tape and a thin steel lighter, strike it on a piece of flint, blow on it and light the wick. Quite a ceremony.

The result was that I quickly developed the picture, washed it and made two prints. A day later we went over to George Bucklin, Consul-General for the U.S. in Guatemala, and showed him. George laughed to hysteria then as suddenly got serious. "Jess, I'm telling you, and it's the truth, in the bar in that hotel two weeks ago, the biggest man in Guatemala, standing 6' 5" and weighing 270 pounds came in there and an Englishman sitting peacefully having a sangría was somehow distasteful and he shot and killed him right at the bar.

"I've made representation to the President to get $5,000, which is usual in this kind of case, for removal of the body and burial but I couldn't get a cent, because feeling is high against the anglo at this time. Now I tell you I want no more blood on my hands. You go from here and take this photograph with you, I don't want it around me; put it in this envelope and do as I say. Go to your hotel, shave clean, catch the train and you will have time to get to Puerto Barrios. There is a United Fruit Co. banana boat loading there today. The shore craft goes back and forth. Give this envelope to the Purser and tell him to put it in the diplomatic pouch, which will come to me and then I will know that you are safely out of the country."

Jesse L. Nusbaum, 1952

"My own acquaintance with Jess Nusbaum began during his service with the
State Museum. Over the years thereafter I had frequent and enjoyable contacts
with him. On occasion, I even traveled by automobile with him in the driver's
seat; his inveterate habit of pointing out things of interest along the way made
this a somewhat scary experience on some of New Mexico's twisting roads.
It is pleasant to report that he seems always to have avoided accidents.
Deep of voice, eloquent, possessed of a robust sense of humor, and one of
the best of companions, the friendship we shared to the day of his death
is one of my most cherished memories. He was a skilled and dedicated
public servant, truly one of the great persons who have given their devotion
to the National Park Service and all the fine things it has always stood for."

S.H. Evison, NPS Historian

Rosemary and Jesse Nusbaum at Uxmal, 1947, "Honeymoon."

*"...to hear a whispered, "here comes Jesse,"
was to sense a man of
more than ordinary charisma."*

Rosemary Nusbaum

The boat on which Jess and Morley went to Tulum (the larger); the smaller craft was one that always came out to meet the larger.

The Young Sylvanus Griswold Morley, "ill on deck," on the way to Tulum.

Sylvanus Morley at Quirigua, Guatemala

Sylvanus L. & Frances Morley, working on field notes at Yaxchilan, 1931.

Uxmal, 1947. Left to right, top row: Rosemary Rife, Frances Morley. Middle row: Tars and Marty, two Morley Hacienda employees; Vay Morley; Rosemary Nusbaum, Mrs. Zoe Stanley. Bottom row: Pastor, a regular helper; Lavinia Rife. This is possibly the last picture taken of Mr. and Mrs. Morley; Vay Morley died in 1948.

Jesse Nusbaum with Mr. Thompson of United Fruit Co., Quirigua, Guatemala, 1911.

Mr. John D. Rockefeller, Jr. on a visit to Santa Fe.
(Photo by Jesse Nusbaum in early 1930s.)

The La Garita Ruins. Photo 1909 by Jesse Nusbaum

The La Garita ruins, 1909; just east of Vay Morley's Santa Fe style house. The Place where Mexican officials assesed and collected excessive fees for permits to sell or trade goods in Santa Fe.

El Ortiz large lounge room, Lamy New Mexico, now demolished. Photo by Jesse Nusbaum, 1912

El Ortiz, Lamy, New Mexico. Famous little Harvey House Hotel now demolished.
Photos by Jesse Nusbaum, 1912

EXCELSIOR
AUTO-CYCLE

Colorful cartoon by Capt Fred Farnoff of the Mounted Patrol, 1909
Caption reads: "Santa Fe cop who arrested Nusbaum & Grisham at 1.30 am Dec. 16-09.
The expression on his face indicates great determination. Fred Farnoff."

Professor Jess Nusbaum, Las Vegas, New Mexico, 1908. Flash set photo by Jesse Nusbaum

"When I got to Santa fe, I had
the only motorcycle in town...
As a result pretty near everyone
in town knew me."
Jesse Nusbaum

Taos Pueblo, 1914. Photo by Jesse Nusbaum.

"I told him that up north at Taos might be the place...to go...a great Pueblo there up to five stories high..."
Jesse Nusbaum

Taos Pueblo, 1914. Shows long ladder going through Kiva roof. Photo by Jesse Nusbaum.

Cedar & Piñon post pole & firewood haulers - 14 wagons in train - enroute to Taos & Taos Pueblo across sagebrush flat, sw of Taos – 1914. Photo & note by Jesse Nusbaum

The Plaza, Santa Fe, New Mexico, before 1900.

Palace of Governors before restoration.

Palace of the Governors, before restoration, 1909.
Jesse Nusbaum's photo is captioned, "Famous Team of Trotters, Santa Fe, New Mexico."

Interior Room, Palace of the Governors, after restoration

Wallace Springer & Jesse Nusbaum in patio of
Palace of Governors, 1911, during restoration.

General Lee Christmas

Yes, I met a most interesting man while I was working in Quirigua and got to know him well: Lee Christmas. I always felt the "General" had been added because of his exploits. He was an American and an adventurer in the true sense of the word, who knew the south of the border area very well.

He was an engineer on the narrow gauge "Ferreas de Guatemala" railroad that ran from Guatemala City down to Puerto Barrios on the Atlantic side, thence to Quirigua, where we were camped and used to see him going back and forth. Now and then he was the conductor. He was an outstanding fancy boy who had a set of false teeth – all gold. This, plus his personality, made a great hit with the people.

Every once in a while when political matters got a little bit disturbing there, they would come in with a boat from old New Orleans, running in many old surplus army rifles that hadn't seen use for years and years. General Lee Christmas would get a few of his compadres who had served as soldiers with him and they would bring up the little boat they called the "Hornet" to the first port and we always knew it.

The Hornet would sail into port and be met there by the Comandante and about a dozen of his fellows. But Lee always carried a Gatling-gun and machine gunner with him. The gun was an old one with a revolving cluster of barrels that fired once each per revolution and could be rotated and maneuvered from side to side and up and down.

We were at Quirigua when Lee Christmas started his main foray. It was the same performance at each small place: The Comandante would come out with his little group of men and get ready to hold them off. What Lee's gunner then did was mow down several of them with the Gatling, then the rest would come over to join up with Lee Christmas, who would then advance from this place to the next.

He kept building up a mission like this making his destination Tegucigalpa, the Capital of Spanish Honduras. Away he went with his gathering army on that train, now become a revolutionary vehicle. Everytime he came to a small group of habitations the same confrontation happened with the local Comandante. The result of it was he would get clear up to the edge of Tegucigalpa to take it and I remember this well, they got one hell of a big rain along the Rio Matagua, which tied and slowed things up and meanwhile an opposing force had time to gather strength and defeated him and Tegucigalpa was not taken.

I used to see him quite a while after this defeat and talk with him, as I had to go back and forth down to Virginia, the station of the United Fruit Company, from Quirigua to Guatamala City.

One day riding on that train I sat next to a comely, well-breasted native girl, and I talked to her in English as we sat on those little old cane seats and she told me she was Mrs. Lee Christmas.

A member of "Ferreas de Guatemala" for whom Christmas worked laughed heartily when I once spoke of this encounter with the lady and said, "Oh, Lee has them in every Port along the Atlantic and in every station all the way up to Guatemala City."

Part II: THE DEEPER SONG

Sylvanus Griswold (Vay) Morley
The Tuxtla Figure

Rosemary met Vay Morley in Chicago shortly after he had married Frances Rhoads of Rock Island, Illinois. Between his seasonal restoration work at Chichen Itzá he gave lectures about the country for the Carnegie Institution of Washington. Short of stature, slight, sandy haired, grey eyed, he came of partial Belgian stock. Since Rosemary's ancestors were Belgian too, she always believed it had bearing on the fine and warm friendship our family enjoyed with him.

He was very myopic and stumbled rather frequently. One time in 1931 at Yaxchilan (that year was the 14th Central American Expedition to the ruins of Yaxchilan in the State of Chiapas, Mexico under the auspices of the Carnegie Institution), he was sitting on a sheltered small portal with one of Frances' stocking-ends cut and tied to form a skull cap for his unruly hair. As he sat working on field notes so oblivious to everything about him a long snake crawled across the floor and over his feet unnoticed. It was a typical incident. He was a rare and brilliant egoist, equally at home with sophisticates as with intellectuals, diplomats or just home folks. Any hostess was assured of a successful dinner if this colorful, warm and witty man were a guest.

We fell into the mutual pleasure of Sunday picnics in various beautiful places on the outskirts of Santa Fe or surrounding villages. In truth they were seminars, sounding boards for his theories. Frances and he liked the outdoors and after the tropics, the climate of Santa Fe stimulated them.

He was an early riser, sometimes phoning the house asking for one of the girls, saying: "I hear you have been naughty, you'd better get that pillow in your breeches because I'm coming right up." There would follow a sqealing scramble to make sure the candy jar was filled to brimming with the colored jelly beans he carried for years. Young Rosemary might remark, "Uncle Vanus has lots of adrenalin in his blood!."

At Uxmal he said to me, "Egyptology fascinates me; I'd love to have had a go at it, but I decided on the Maya field about the same time Jess couldn't get *Early Man in America* out of his system." He spoke often of the great art and beauty of the Egyptians. He was constantly searching and thinking and as a result was completely in love with the whole world. I played a trick on him in the early years and everytime he thought about it, it sent him out of his chair, walking the floor with that pained look on his face while twisting his cowlick of hair. Then he would stop in front of my chair and say: "Goddamn you, Jess Nusbaum, you let me make a damned fool of myself in front of all those eminent scientists." Much laughter and story-telling would always follow.

While excavating in 1909 at Rito de los Frijoles Canyon under Hewett, Morley was on a kick of wondering if the Maya were not in some ethnological way connected with the early Indians here. He dreamed a lot and talked little while digging, so we began asking him questions and kidding him as he worked in fits and starts. He would sit and he would start talking, caught up with this idea. I would finish a whole room before he was a third through the parallel one he was working on.

Well, Vay began describing this thing and someone would ask him something about it, then Chap (Kenneth M. Chapman, artist, pottery expert) would question him. Next thing we found Vay thought, should be a statuette of jade, a Tuxtla (one of the earliest possible contemporaneously dated objects), and he thought it would be about six inches high. Soon he had given us a complete description and we got Chap to help us and we carved pieces of cottonwood root, which people used to make Kachinas. The root is soft and has no grain so it cuts well and doesn't split.

Without letting Vay see us we started carving and every time we were uncertain, we'd let another fellow talk to Vay so he'd describe it in fuller detail. Finally, we were working on the face of a cliff. There were a series of rooms about 300 feet high on two levels. The cavaté ones were cut out of rock and the outer ones built against it. I had the room to the left of where Vay was excavating, Chap on the other side and others working too, all aimed toward the last row to get to the cliff. I was finishing along to the end of my room, when I noted pretty near to the cliff wall a ventilator opening where the "early ones" used a plug to aereate between two rooms. It's usually a small hole with a tufa-plug to close it off.

At last we had the Tuxtla faked to our satisfaction. All colored by Chap, we buried it in the horse corral to get a proper odor of age and so it looked good and old. When I found the ventilator hole I knew I could reach right down through, get the faked Tuxtla up into the corner of the next room, then get the place packed with loose sand and get the plug back in, cave it a little down so I'd be working on the other side of the room.

Vay was now three feet from getting up to the hole in his room. I was certain he did not know what I was up to, so all was set and the next day the fellows began telling him, "My God, Vay, look how far you are, why you're not... why we're all going to be finished here before you get up there." So Vay worked and talked about the parrot feathers we had found earlier and how certain he was that they had somehow come from Maya country, that the turquoise in Mexico had been retrieved from near Cerrillos and that the Rito de los Frijoles was not much farther.

All of a sudden about 4 p.m. Vay exclaimed for all to hear, "Allah! Allah! Allah!" and bumped his head to the ground repeating, "Allah!"

We all got over there to see what was up and there was Vay, with the front of this thing just showing and Vay getting ready to take the rest of the dirt away from it. This done, he picked it up and cradled it in his arms just like it was a newborn babe and took it down to camp, where he showed it to Dr. Hewett, Ed Springer and Chas Lummis and the whole gang down there.

That night they got him to talk about it as we all sat around for an hour listening to his premise that this proved the very thing...there was not a peep out of any of us. Drs. Hewett and Springer were not in on our miserable deception. Vay got away with it for some weeks but finally we had to let the goose out. He went about in misery saying, "Hey, hey, you let me get up there and make a damned fool of myself before all those noted archaeologists and I don't know why I never questioned it, 'cause I knew it wasn't jade." But he always admired the accurate wooden deception for its figure and even the glyph.

I'd fool him a lot. Often we'd pick up a tufa block and throw it back and forth as we passed it along. I'd get a good sized block, soak it in Frijoles creek and water-log it, let it dry a little then throw a little dust on it and when it came my turn I'd toss it to Vay. Being little, it would tip him end over end.

La Garita

From June 1909 on, with the organization of the School of American Archaeology and the Museum of New Mexico, the staff became the principal public spokesmen for the preservation and perpetuation of architectural traditions of the past. Joined by a group of artists, writers, historians, business leaders and citizens, we created the New-Old Santa Fe Exhibition of 1912.

After this, S.G. Morley began discussing with Jess his desire to restore the ruin of La Garita, the sentry/tribute station and hang-out for political juntas of the area. It stood, starkly crumbling into the past, on the west slope below the acropolis of Fort Marcy. With restoration in mind, Jess had taken many photographs for Morley, who then purchased the land where it stood. He then bought and restored a fine old adobe residence for himself in this area.

The Garita at Santa Fe was not like the sentry garitas one saw when travelling into the interior of Mexico in the States of Zacatecas and Chihuahua. The Mexican counterparts were furnished with towers with loopholes in them through which guns could be poked and observations could be made during disturbances or wartime. The Santa Fe Garita had been diamond shaped with towers at its corners. It stood high and picturesquely commanded a sentinal position for the early trails which led into Santa Fe. The most prominent was from Taos, then the only port of entry for trade for the earliest pack trains all entered from that northern route. The Garita had been built of sun-dried adobe, laid in clay mortar and had no foundation except for perhaps a few stones! Although unused from the time of American occupation, it had been the site of great activity following 1850 when commerce with the prairie states developed in earnest and became increasingly profitable (See: Josiah Gregg, *Commerce of the Prairies.* 1954: University of Oklahoma Press). In 1821, this had been the end of the trail for Indian trader Captain William Becknell. Dubbed "Father of the Santa Fe Trail," he had freighted goods by pack-horses from Missouri across the plains with his four companions, had followed the Cimarron route to San Miguel and on to Santa Fe. Two years later the Spring caravan brought $30,000 of goods to New Mexico; the traders returned to Missouri with $180,000 in gold and silver, $10,000 in furs and the Santa Fe trade route was established.

Colonel Francisco Perea spent the winter of 1837-38 in Santa Fe and wrote of the Garita: "The garita at Santa Fe was a very ordinary structure when compared with the three buildings I saw while travelling in the interior of Mexico." (He referred to the garitas at Chihuahua, Aguas Calientes and Monte Rey.)

In 1932, when the author first saw the Santa Fe Garita, a portion of its thick walls were still standing. One evening at our home, S.G. Morley was explaining his keen desire to restore it and he became so enthusiastic that we drove up to see it. The sun was already setting as, in his articulate way, he painted a word picture of the trails coming in, emphasizing that this was one of the essential historic structures to be preserved. He stated the City of Santa Fe should never overlook the restoration of Fort Marcy, sitting 600 yards above the Palace of the Governors for the same historic reasons.

The shadows grew long as we stood lost in thoughts of the past. The old cemetery with its crumbling low adobe walls lay below and to the north. The earthen works of the old fort above were still completely evidenced. But the tall gramma grasses, usually stirring in the early wind of evening, were silent as were the chamisa, golden and heavy with late Summer's bloom, growing from other seasons when the deep wagon trails marring the hillsides had been made. The sounds that had made them, and the voices were now all stilled by time.

In 1979 as this is written, all that remains is a small section of crude stone reinforcement that can yet be seen on the north corner of a shallow arroyo as you drive east up Kearney Avenue, where the old Garita once stood.

LA GARITA

High by the side of the trail it stood
Right well on the way toward Taos
And it wound right on, through the Cimarron
To cross the plains of the west.

From Dodge City the cowboy town
Came the couriers with merchants and trade
To be assessed; to tell the news
And live 'til the spirit was spent.

So proud, on the height by the trail it was built
A marker for stern mountain-men
The shade of its walls, could resound with the calls
Of a Carson, or Kearney or Bent.

'Tis now but a mound of broken brown earth
Indeed 'tis a frail dreary sight
With only the winds to kindle the sod
And the rains to fall overall.

Rosemary Nusbaum

Bryan Boru Dunne and the Badger

When I was working on the restoration of the Palace of the Governors, a man blew in here, the brother of a prominent judge in Baltimore. He had gone into the newspaper business and had come here to sell the town on the idea of getting out a special addition of the *New Mexican* that would contain much advertising plus local interest.

He came in and bothered me all the time for things he wanted. Knowing next to nothing about the country around here he demanded photographs of current events, people and areas. He was strident and persistent and since I was a public servant — and in the interest of the town — I helped him. About this time a fellow from down Lamy way came in and it was announced in the paper that he had just caught the biggest badger ever seen and had brought it into town saying, "Why, this badger can lick even the largest bulldog ever lived!"

As often happened during this period a Minstrel Show came through and advertised a performance to be held at the Elks Theater on Lincoln Avenue. It was called "Honey Boy Evans and His Famous Minstrels." Now, Honey Boy was a big fella who wore a big long theatrical coat in that warm autumn weather, and spats on his shoes and everything colorful. The group was anglo but played black-face and called themselves names appropriate to this type show such as Sambo or Bones. Believe it or not, Honey Boy also owned a bulldog that travelled with him. This canine wore a royal purple coat embellished with spangles and gold braid and was always on a leash, leading out. Now this Lamy fellow kept repeating the threat that the badger "could lick any bulldog ever lived." When Honey Boy heard this, he challenged the badger-owner, so it was arranged that after the Minstrels performed that night we would all journey up to the Masonic Hall...then on the southside of the Plaza over Moore's mens store. The hall consisted of a large kitchen, dining room on one side with swinging doors into the lodge-room.

That evening a very glowing article appeared in the paper by B.B. Dunne on how I'd given him a very educational lecture on the badger including his life-cycle and habits. Gus Koch and Frank Keefe ran a modern grocery store then on the corner where the First National Bank now stands and they were able to provide a large solid wooden box to hold the big badger and they helped fix it up with a strap so you could raise the front end very quickly then control it with you foot. Then they found an old fashioned enamel "thunder mug." Frank Keefe provided some old browned bananas and they put in some stale beer and lastly a chain was attached on it for a hold. Because of the newspaper article, so many people came over to see this contest that quite a bit of betting had been going on and tensions were already high.

None of Honey Boy's group had seen the badger, but the build up had been so big they were ready to bite on anything. Their lady followers all came up with them to join the others. It was decided that because of the large number of men in the kitchen and dining room, the ladies should go to the lodge room.

Because of heightened interest they decided someone neutral had to hold the chain. Almost everyone laid a bet on the Minstrel's bulldog and finally they turned to B.B. Dunne who, when asked, stated he'd made no bet. "Alright," they said, "you get out here." So B.B. pulled on the fancy yellow gloves, tightened his big well-worn tan western hat and wound the chain protruding from the box several times around his waist. The bulldog was brought in, well-leashed, to stand beside the box where every little while one of the men would kick the box and the bulldog sniffed and barked and tension really got high.

No one had yet seen the badger, which was silent in the dark box, and no one admitted ever having seen a badger fight. Anticipation rose. At this point B.B. Dunne announced he had never seen a badger, he was mighty afraid of 'em, and that he had been told this badger weighed over 30 pounds. He faced away when the "ready" was called. Someone kicked the bulldog which began barking. B.B. never looked back, he made one dive through the swinging doors that led from the kitchen into the lodge room, splashing bananas and beer after him. People started yelling; women screamed and there was amazement to be sure. B.B., his bed-chamber on the end of the chain splashing away, made a full circle of the room. He was mighty upset when he found out the whole story. He came to me to complain "You have ruined me socially in this town, ruined me socially!"

"Why did you drag it in there in front of the women? Why didn't you keep it in the kitchen?" I asked. He said, "I had to get away—that bulldog was after me!"

Ever after this he referred to me as "that Elijah and his chariot of fire," because of my motorcycle.

The day after the badger fight, Honey Boy and his troupe of about 15 left town for Lamy to board the train. He wore his long lavender coat, light colored spats and cane, fancy high plug hat and the bulldog, leading out on his leash.

At Lamy, the finishing touches were just being put on the little hotel down there and they were trying to find a proper name for it. Someone suggested Los Pinos (the pines). A plasterer I was using here was just putting those letters on and molding them in securely on the front. The "L" was bannerlike on the lovely carved strip over the window. Jerry Black, the passenger traffic manager for the Santa Fe Railroad, and Ed Wine were there to observe. As Honey Boy walked up with a girl on his arm, he stood there for a moment, then pointed his cane and exclaimed, "Found at last!" Someone asked "What?" And he answered, "the lost penis." With that, Jerry Black got so fussed he said, "Get that damned thing down before it sets." Everyone had a great laugh. About three months later the new hotel was named "El Ortiz."

Rosemary, you remember Dunne very well. You used to talk about the little black book he carried for years where he made notes about important visitors to La Fonda and how he could be found in the lobby most of the time. All those things were delightful, as was the Santa Fe Club when it existed on Washington Street where Santa Fe National Bank now stands. Bronson Cutting was one of its promoters and I joined as did Vay Morley, Carl Bishop, Harry Dorman, Sam Cartwright, Ted Espy, Levi Hughes and Dr. Massey to name a few. Ladies could come only as guests, so when there was a party and there were strong drinks for the men, the women would complain we gave them "dishwater." They often spiked it up and the place became quite a status symbol.

There was an occasional full-dress affair when we all wore tie and tails. About this time Louise Pugh came here to buy a place across from Hal Bynner's (poet/writer, Witter Bynner) place on Buena Vista. When I was teaching at Las Vegas Normal University, she used to ride horseback from Watrus to come into the Casteñeda for a weekly bath and would then sit out on the front porch, put her booted feet up on the rail and rock in a rocking chair, always boasting that her folks had money.

You told me, Rosemary, you would see her at Bynner's parties which he often gave then for visitors such as Rose O'Neill of kewpie-doll fame. You recalled seeing the artist John Sloan and his wife Dolly and Will Shuster there. We both found the evenings at Bynner's an educational adventure with his guests participating in the entertainment. Hal was always ready for a party since he slept much of the day and worked all night. Sloan and Shuster would put on their mirthful telephone conversation between two "native" girls and Hal would read us some of his poetry.

I often stopped over to visit Jack Nairn at his home on the Waite Phillips ranch, now the famous Boy Scout Ranch. I met Jack in Washington D.C. when he lived in the nearest house to the White House across from the Treasury Building (1909). He was famous then for his Southern dialect he had learned from a negro mammy and used to be invited to the White House to tell stories. His father was a minister there and had bought real estate that became valuable.

Jack had gone to Texas with a desire to acquire a ranch. Being an excellent horseman and trainer he was hired on the strength of his fast "polo." They kidded him a good deal, but there wasn't a mean horse they could put him on that he couldn't ride. They tell of the time he went to San Antonio and attended a grand dinner in the old Buckhorn Bar there. The place was noted for the long mahogany table out front where the locals like to eat. On this particular night there occurred all the trimmings of fine silver and crystal. A great spread, with the ladies wearing their finest dresses and diamonds. At one point a Texan arose to give a toast but the words would not come. Jack stood, raised his arm and said, "I'll give it." Then lifting his glass high over his head he continued, "Hells afloat and the devil's a swimmin' —Goddamned the man that doesn't like wimmin." A roar went up from the crowd.

A Motorcycle Cop for the Ancient City

I started to use a motorcycle in Greeley before 1900... a one and a quarter horsepower Indian with a chain drive. It didn't have a clutch and for speed I had to run and push it pretty hard to warm it up and get it started. The engine on it was right where the post comes up and the damned thing would get so hot, it could burn the knees out of your pants.

Then I got an Excelsior and broke the dirt road record in 1908, beating the passenger car travel by three hours from Denver to Las Vegas, New Mexico. The only place I wasn't shaken up was on the rail-bed, because the ties were set even and flat. Everytime I switched tracks I had to pick up the motorcycle and carry it over, but I got down there by finally pushing it halfway over Raton Pass and it was pretty steep. The old belt drive would slip and burn if you let it, so I'd get off and run, push then hop on for a short way, then run again.

When I got to Santa Fe, I had the only motorcycle in town and there were only five automobiles. I got around in it going to the old penitentiary south of town for brick and lime when I was working on the Palace of the Governors, and again when building the Art Museum. As a result pretty near everyone in town knew me.

An ordinance was passed by the City fathers for the control of traffic, which permitted one to drive four miles per hour, going from the Plaza west down San Francisco and on down Don Gaspar. Eight miles an hour was permitted around the Plaza and 12 miles a maximum in any other part of Santa Fe. Two other laws were passed at this time: (1) A driver travelling at night on any vehicle or sort of conveyance had to have a warning signal which must be heard 100 yards ahead, and also a head light or a lantern.

At this time Brian Boru Dunne rode horseback so he came along carrying a lantern in one hand. Sam Failor, a tinsmith, tied his lantern on the rear axel of a little buggy he drove around in, so I had to get something.

Mrs. Mary Bradford Prince, wife of a former governor, was still looked up to as the doyenne of the town. She was raising so much hell about it all and it seemed could not be pleased. Kinda seemed unnecessary, so I sent a wire up to Perry Mead in Denver telling him I wanted the shrillest sounding device you could adapt on a motorcycle and could be mounted on it. They replied that they had "just the thing" called a "spectrophone," making a shrill crying sound that could be heard a half mile. I said "send it," then I put it on.

Shortly thereafter, Mary Prince went to a meeting of the City Council and had a fellow name of J.H. Parks, Superintendent of Education for the State of New Mexico, make a statement saying, "Jess Nusbaum has a motorcycle equipped with the shrillest, shrieking, crying ever heard and I have confirmed that three women have suffered miscarriages after hearing that horn."

After I had made sure that this had been said, one afternoon I happened to be coming down Palace Avenue with one girl sitting on the tank on the handlebars in front, and Dotty Hoskins on the platform behind me. I let them off at their series of rooms in the Prince Plaza on Palace and as I continued down Palace I saw Mary Prince, who weighed all of 200 pounds. As always, she was wearing her black shiny silk-rustling taffeta dress and her customary little hat.

There she was toddling along at the northeast corner of the Plaza. I had a cut-out on the muffler and when you pulled it out it made a hell of a roar; then if I retarded the spark and with compression it made a loud bang-bang like noise. Well, it was too much. Just as I got behind Mary I let 'er go. When I glanced back there was just a swoon in the middle of the street, right in the dust, a little hat sitting on top of a black pile. I went directly to the west gate of the Governor's Palace and took off that horn and got out of there quick.

After this I was picked up on some pretext. I challenged it and they appointed me the City's first motorcycle cop. I never did arrest anyone and my commission soon died.

Of Taos and Amigos

I've told you stories, Rosemary, about Maurice Stern, the artist who was once married to Mabel Lujan. Stern became a friend when I met him while working at the Museum of the American Indian, Heye Foundation in New York City. He liked to paint the colorful Blackfeet Indians around Crater Lake. I considered him a very good artist. I'd met him at the home of my good friends Joseph and Margery Asche; Asche had become a famous M.D. I remember well that it was a musicale at which the noted violinist Mischa Elman played and a Steinway had been especially brought in for his accompanist.

Maurice came into the Heye Museum confiding that he would like to get out West to paint. He wanted to get to conservative Indians; ones who were difficult to paint and whose portraits had not been painted before. "Well," I told him, "I think I have an idea where just the best place would be for you to go, where the Indians do not want their people painted and do not welcome outsiders coming in to question them about their rights and ways. A people who are proud individualists."

He replied, "I'd like that, for its the sort of thing I'd do." When I asked him what else he had done and where he had travelled, he told me he and his wife Mabel took time off each year to roam all over the world and never stayed at home for long periods.

I asked him what she liked and he replied that she liked Italy "and is strong for that; she loves the sea, mountains, skies, clouds and trees." I told him that up north at Taos might be a place for him to go. "There's a great Pueblo there up to five stories high and the Indians are colorful and picturesque. Why don't you ask her out."

"Mabel," he replied, "has never been west of Yonkers about 40 miles up the Hudson from New York City where we have a big 17 room house we have lived in for several years. It is jam-packed with art and things we have bought all over the world and its been shipped there. We have an arrangement. She buys one week and I buy the next and all this collection is back there." I replied, "Taos will just suit her fine then; you can build up there with adobes, the help is very cheap and you can build a lot for a little. Get her to look the place over. Bring her out."

Well, he did and he painted at Santo Domingo. He had a big car. A Lozier, which hung low to the ground. The dirt road down there was just two troughs where the wheels went and the teams, with a high centered ridge.

Next time I went out that way on my motorcycle I found where someone had to dig a car out...holes where a car had been hung up. Maurice said he had constantly gotten hung up on the straddle. He'd dug out to get started on the road again to paint at Santo Domingo.

Some months later I was back in New York again when Maurice came to see me. I asked, "What are you doing here, I'd heard you were at Taos with Mabel, and painting?"

"Oh, you suggested I get my wife Mabel out — well, we're living in the Manby house. She has just sent me back."

"Why?" I asked.

"She's buying up land in Taos and she has started to build. She's building houses all over that place. Very elaborate ones. Fixing up everything and getting ready to have all her furniture and collections up there. I'm here to get a carload of it off and ready to go. There will be several."

For several years thereafter while I was Superintendent of the Mesa Verde National Park, Mabel would come up with friends and always one Taos Indian in particular, named Tony. They would spend about three days at a time up there, go about in her private car and have all meals served in their cabin, not mixing with the public and obviously enjoying the ruins.

One year Mabel came with a very wealthy woman from Buffalo. Tony was driving and there was also a very good looking young Indian with them. Mabel was doing her darndest to interest the young man in this woman, to get an Indian for herself. From Mesa Verde they went to the Apache dances at Stone Lake on the Jicarilla Reservation. Dr. Martin (T.P. Martin, Taos physician) told me later than when they got back to Taos he was in attendance at a big goodbye dinner with this foursome. The other woman had fallen in love with Tony and following the dinner she was loudly heard to say: "Mabel, this is my last night here and tonight is the night you pass the buck."

Mabel finally married Tony, and a friend of mine in Boston who was on the board of Harvard University saw a notice in the Boston *Globe* that day where Mabel Dodge Sterne had married Antonio Lujan, a full-blooded Taos Indian at Taos, New Mexico. Edwin Dodge, a Bostonian, was sitting in a large leather chair, in the sedate Century Club and noting his presence, my friend took the paper over to him, read the notice and asked comment. Dodge hardly looked up as he dryly remarked, "Lo! the poor Indian."

Mabel had been a hell-raiser up at Buffalo. She had a pony cart up there and drove about in outré dress shocking people. She loved it. After she married Tony, they used to come to New York and she would take a place where she continued to entertain the celebrities and aesthetes of the day...Tony always with his hair beautifully done in braids and wearing full Indian costume.

Tony was bored with her continuous debate with sex and life and would come to the Museum. On one of these trips he saw a peyote set, very complete with the fans and all. He wanted this above all else and came to me. "I'd like to have the whole outfit, we don't have it. It would make it much better."

I questioned, "But you don't use peyote up there?"

46

"Yes," he said. "Taos has a ceremony but not this kind of set. Mabel belongs to the peyote clan and so do I. We have a regular cult up there."

He tried many days to get this outstanding set that Mark Harrington (archaeologist) had picked up in the Ozarks of Oklahoma, where they had lots of it. Here was the whole thing, the shield, fans, buttons. Mark had gotten in with the peyote people of the Ozarks when he was collecting down there for the Museum of the American Indian (Heye Foundation). One day George Heye, the director, had gotten a call telling him, "You had better send someone down here to get your man, I fear he has been on a peyote feast." And he had been. Harrington used to tell me about it and would get so darned excited and clear beside himself about the colors and patterns. But he had gotten horribly sick afterward. Tony never got it.

When Mabel acquired other male interests she would give Tony $500 and he would take the young ones on trips. She always provided him with a good car and Tony seemed to enjoy this.

Mabel tried to divorce Tony at one time and she went to an attorney friend of mine, but the Judge refused her saying, "Mabel, you came up here and stole Tony from his wife and finally married him; now you want a divorce and as long as I am Judge you will never get it." Mabel pleaded, offering a very substantial settlement to Tony's Indian wife. The Judge, a friend of mine, told me he had said, "Very well, Tony's ex-wife owns her home at the Pueblo; its a nice little place there. If she were to get a lump settlement, some young buck would go over and make love to her and she would lose her money. You, Mabel will pay her $35 each month as long as she lives and guarantee this." So it was worked out this way.

About the peyote, though: Remember, Rosemary, we visited Victor Higgins (the Taos artist) in his studio, which was one of Mabel's guest houses? Victor told us, "Well, being an artist, I was intensely curious and felt I might learn something of colors, to be revealed for my work and I tried peyote once. The kaleidoscope of forms and colors were fantastic, but the effect was so drastic on me that I would never have dared try it again." Victor spoke freely of the use of peyote among a certain group of Indians up there.

T.P. Martin, the physician up there in Taos ministered to most of the artists. I used to go up to see him and it was fun to accompany him on several occasions when he made country calls. His dog, "Tides" sat in a hand-made box on the side of the little dinky car he drove. Tides was a white bulldog and seemed to know that country as well as his master. One day we visited seven pairs of twins. Later when he went to make a speech in St. Louis he told the gathered medics that his secret with children was the milk of the female burro. He had collected an extensive collection of Santos and Bultos, and many were later sold to Nolie Mumey (a surgeon) of Denver.

47

Mabel did a surprising thing — she went off to the Public Work's Program people, saying she felt kind of sorry for Tony living out there in his little house with no place to care for nature's necessities and she did not like his having to go out in the corral behind the fence and would like him to have the comforts others were getting. She had them build this special Chick-Sale (outdoor toilets of wood built by the Public Works) and set it up for him at the Pueblo.

Mabel simply followed along as she did when she developed an association with D.H. Lawrence, who had a wife named Frieda. Frieda was the daughter of a Prussian officer and had been the Baroness Elsa von Freytag von Loringhoven, wife of this wealthy German Businessman. When Lawrence came to Taos, Mabel thought he was coming alone, and she had put a double bed in his room. But he brought Frieda and Mabel promptly sent her maids over there and made it a single and attempted to assign Frieda to other quarters in that part of her property which was strung out into a series of single rooms. Frieda stuck like a leach for a time but found Mabel too much.

I never though Mabel pretty. She wore her dark hair down; sometimes bangs. She was not witty but had a talent for attracting people of heavy philosophical differences and for writing. She would write to a notable person and bring up a subject she knew they felt strongly about. They would answer and she would publish it in the paper.

She could be quite a tyrant, although in later years 'twas said she mellowed somewhat. The very proper Hazel Pond then living in Taos became quite fond of Mabel and once said to me: "Mabel confessed to me that she embellished events because she knew the value of this in the markets." At one period in Taos Mabel carried on a lengthy correspondence with George Bernard Shaw and brought up some testy things. He in turn tried to explain them whereupon Mabel would publish them. Shaw once made a trip to Taos, but stayed only a short time and made caustic remarks about it.

I look back with pleasure on the summer visits we used to have from Mr. Farwell of Texas and Judge Hamlin. Hamlin was at this time still working out details of the land deal in which the Busch family of Chicago were involved with the University of Texas. It was an extensive gift of some 40 miles of land, involving ten counties rich with oil and gas and caused much comment here.

Farwell and Hamlin were great friends of Harriett Rolshoven and Mabel Hall and they used the La Fonda as a summer retreat. These extremely wealthy and pleasant Texans had a favorite table at the left entrance of the outside patio and could be found lunching there almost every noon. It was said that they knew more about Santa Feans than they knew about themselves!.

One day Hamlin went up to see T.P. Martin in Taos as he frequently visited the art world up there. On this occasion he asked T.P. what he might see and was told: "Mabel is having one of her 'blow-outs' tonight." Hamlin confided:

"You know Doc, I never had an affair with an Indian." "Well," replied T.P., "I'm going over and I'll take you and introduce you, but I'm not staying. There will be young women from the Pueblo serving food and her parties usually run pretty late, so don't be too noisy when you come in. I'll need some sleep. Good Luck."

Late that evening Hamlin wandered out on the dimly lighted porch to sit on the swing. Pretty soon a very cordial person with long dark hair came and sat beside him. They got to playing around a bit and to the Judge's great shock, he found he was sitting beside a man. He was still snorting when he got back and wakened Doc, who asked: "How'd you do?" "Oh, my God!" he replied. "A horrible mess. I thought I had one but it was a man."

About this time Carter Harrison, then mayor of Chicago used to come up to Taos and one night they were kidding him: "Carter" they asked: "How are you going to put yourself over with the colored people in your speech next week before the prestigious Cliff Dwellers Club? It ends your re-election campaign and you know it's usually the colored vote that puts you over."

"Well," he said, "We'll see."

Some of his friends attended as Carter addressed this famous Club on the South side telling the audience that indeed he had an uncle who had gone to darkest Africa..."and who knows?" Carter won again.

Part III: THE ANCIENT CITY
Santiago and the "Big Hot"

Santiago Naranjo, whose Indian name is K'hapóa ("Masterkey"), five times Governor of the Santa Clara Pueblo, situated along the Rio Grande near Española, New Mexico, a real patriarch, was my guide and handled the burro and cooked for me on the first archaeological exploration in 1908, when I photographed all the then-known ruins on the Pajarito Plateau.

As the years passed I wanted to get my great friend to see Mesa Verde, because he had said he would like to. He always said, "Well, I can't go. I have to look after my people." One Sunday when Santiago was about 80 years old, I went down to the Plaza and saw him sitting on the Art Museum porch about 2 o'clock in the afternoon. I went over and said, "Santiago, what are you doing?"

"Oh," he answered, "I'm just sitting around."

I said, "How about going with me over to Gallup and then to the Grand Canyon, and you can see the great canyon high bridge. Then I'm going to Zion and then head back through beautiful red country. I'll stop at Chaco Canyon and I'll show you Pueblo Bonito." He looked thoughtful as I continued. "Have you ever been west of Gallup?" "No," he answered. I said, "Hop in." "Well, I'll have to let my daughter know." I said, "Telephone to Juan Naranjo's store up there." He answered, "Sunday, no telephone. He's not there." I said, "Then we'll leave a note with Gladys Jenkins of the courier staff at La Fonda and she will take it out to your daughter." Then I added, "I'll take you back to the Pueblo on Thursday." So we left the note as he wrote it with Gladys and he got in with me.

When we got to Gallup — he had been there before — he was very happy. I got him a room with a bath and after a good dinner he came into the lobby, where he sang and told stories, much to the delight of visitors.

He had been pretty soiled when we started and the next morning to my startled eyes, he came down with the beaver fur in his hair all matted and wet; he was all shining and clean and still pink. I asked, "What did you do last night?"

"Oh," he said, "I went up to the room." I asked, "Then what did you do?"

"Oh," he answered, "I was long while in the big hot." He had been in the tub for a long while and had washed everything.

As we proceeded, a man his age feels the need of the call of nature once in a while and he wanted to stop. As long as we were clear out in the open and no cars anyway, I would stop. Finally, when we got up toward the Gap, before we got to the canyon, he wanted to stop once again and I said, "No, we are going to Jerry O'Farrel's big trading post — great big building there, we will eat there — curio store — big house on this side, big house on the other and you go there...'him' on one side, 'her' on the other side." We drove along and got there.

I had a lot of gear in the car so I wanted to lock up. He walked over to the "him" house. I didn't see whether he went in because I was closing the car. Just then a big car, a great big black limousine, liveried chauffeur and all, came in. Two fine aristocratic, white-haired ladies, California license, looked like they might be from San Francisco, drove up and stopped right next to us. As they started to get out of their car I thought I heard a characteristic sound against the building and I looked around there, and there was Santiago relieving himself.

I almost whispered, "Whoof, whoof, Santi-ag-o, no, no, women, women, women."

With that he slowly looked at me with the greatest disdain and he said, "When an Indian has got to, an Indian's going to ." I asked him why he hadn't gone into the building.

He said, "Door locked."

PAJARITO

As I walked over the Mesa today
A field of turquoise lupine broke as a sea.
And all about me far and near—
Like the wake of a great wave's spray
The virgin mariposa lily's bloomed.

And as I thought this vision fair to see
I came upon a lizard dozing in the Sun:
Who vanished, like some disembodied sprite
Leaving his tail behind.

Then, looking up to follow sound
I saw jet-planes arranged in flight
Sparkling, beautious they seemed to hang,
Then suddenly detached from the sky—
Left for me a vapor trail.

Rosemary Nusbaum

Matilda Coxe Stevenson and the Zuni

Colonel Stevenson was a very famous anthropologist with the Bureau of American Ethnology and he came down to work at Zuni. When he died his wife Matilda (see *Indian Blankets and their Makers*, George W. James, page 141) stayed there and worked for 23 years. Her large report of this work became the noted *Twenty-Third Annual Report of the Bureau of American Ethnology.*

She once came up to Santa Fe and John P. Harrington (the noted ethnologist and linguist) was here and knew her. Mrs. Prince heard that they were here and invited Tillie Stevenson over. Mrs. Prince weighed about 200 pounds and Tillie maybe 210. Harrington was also at this party and had gotten into full dress "putting on the dog" he told me when I arrived, as did others.

Sara, the Prince maid, was dressed up and letting us all in and the host, the former Governor, Bradford L. Prince, was much in evidence with his fine growth of whiskers. It was quite a party and as I stood with Harrington at one point, Tillie was talking with Mrs. Prince as they moved over to join us.

Mrs. Prince was asking, "Did the Indians have any name for you?"

"Oh, yes," responded Tillie softly, "They always called me mother."

Harrington asked, "As you know, I am a linguist and I'd like to know what word the Zunis used for mother?"

Tillie answered "Po-pog-ha-ii." At that Harrington sputtered and turned quickly to get out of there. Wondering what the blazes it was, I went over and asked him. He answered red faced:

"It means the old fat woman with the big flat anus."

John P. Harrington was a constant worker who had long periods of gastric problems. About this time Kenneth Chapman went to see him. He told Chap he never took time to eat but would throw a few mutton chops on the open fire and when crisp and burned he ate them, "as black bits flying all over."

Chap said, "I'll telephone over to Andrew's Grocery down here on San Francisco Street. They sell fine Zwiebach. I use it all the time and I'll get you a five-pound bottle of Horlick's malted milk. They will deliver it all and I'll come over later and fix it up for you the first time. You will find as I do that it will keep you together."

That evening he went over and found Harrington all doubled up on the couch in horrible shape. He had eaten it all.

Panama Pacific Exposition, San Diego, 1915

I had quit Hewett and went to work as builder of the "Painted Desert" Pueblo structures, for the Atchison, Topeka & Santa Fe Railway Company. They needed somebody who could do it and came to me; thus I became director of the Painted Desert exhibit for the 1915 Santa Fe Railway/Panama Pacific Exposition.

Knowing the Indians, I followed their desires in the architecture and combined my plans of what I thought appropriate and authentic to the occasion. Mary J. Colter (decorator) did one small model. She was very talented but I worked from photographs I'd taken in the Southwest. I got 23 Indian friends and workers from San Ildefonso Pueblo, most I had known from my work at Puyé and Rito de los Frijoles and we created the "Two Cities of the Desert." They worked along with me and we built quite a monument as tier upon tier went up to scrape the San Diego sky. I used stone, wood and adobe, thatched after the manner of the old Indians. I used ladders and achieved the wild, weird and strange impression that visitors always felt on first coming to the Southwest.

It became an ethnological exhibit of uncommon human interest, that could have housed and cared for 100 inhabitants. It had a trading post and small kiva. They wove blankets, prepared their food, made artistic ornaments, pottery in their accustomed manner, to the fascination and pleasure of the numberless visitors who listened to their music and songs, beheld their colorful dances and wondered what religious ceremonials took place in their underground kiva.

The Railway provided transportation for them which was a delightful experience and they enjoyed the ocean. There seemed to be something of the Great Spirit — the great intelligence compatible with their complete respect for nature about it to them and this was reflected as entire families settled into this pueblo-like home on the Pacific. I trained them to help me run the display; it went well. My job had been to seize the relic of time, to transport it and this I did with their cooperation. Maria, Julian and Macimina (Martinez family, famous potters) came from the Pueblo in April and stayed until the fair ended in January.

"Hopi Smith" an anglo, ran the Hopi House at the Grand Canyon and did the same at the fair and he managed the Hopi dancers, who came out several times each day to dance for the visitors. It never failed to bring a new kind of pleasure and excitement to all. I noted that some people came back many times. Smith finally asked for more Hopis and the Governor of San Ildefonso also thought his people had been away from their pueblo long enough. So it was the Hopis took over and my work being long completed, I went to work with Herman Schweizer of the Fred Harvey Company in Albuquerque for the next six months, to set up the famous Indian room at the Alvarado Hotel.

Honorable Frank Springer

As time passed the "Painted Desert" structures I built at San Diego have often been confused with the New Mexico Building at the exposition, which I had nothing to do with, 'tho I thought it a beautiful composite on a smaller scale of the Mission and Convento at Acoma, New Mexico.

Frank Springer was a great friend of Edgar Hewett. He came out to San Diego to see the fair after I had completed the "Painted Desert," and was tremendously pleased with what I had done saying, "It's the finest thing I've ever seen."

After he got back to Santa Fe, he promptly wrote me that Hewett had gotten him more interested in the art end of the Museum and they had decided they must have an Art Museum in Santa Fe. He asked me to make certain beyond any question of doubt, one year ahead of any construction of such an edifice, that I would be available to accept the position of Superintendent of Construction, and meantime asked me to work on the architectural features compatible with this possibility.

The Honorable Frank Springer was a brilliant man of many facets and talents: Lawyer, artist and world renowned authority on Crinoids and always a friend of the arts. I'd met his son Wallace while teaching at Las Vegas, New Mexico in 1907-1908 and we were later roommates through the College Session at George Washington University. I was working for my tuition with the great W.H. Holmes (of the National Museum in Washington, D.C.) making casts and case-molds at the National Museum. My old malaria came back in that climate and I returned to the University of Colorado for the Summer Session in 1914.

Pecos

I was still with Schweizer when coming down on the train one day to Santa Fe, I chanced to meet Hewett. He approached me with, "Jess, you are just the man I've got to have. A.V. Kidder (then Field Director for Phillips Academy, Andover, Mass.) is due soon to excavate at Pecos for interested organizations and persons and I think you are the man we want to go up there to investigate and stabilize the basal-walls of the Mission." He offered me $150 per month, plus $370 for workmen and materials. It was more than I was making, and knowing something of the Mission, I accepted.

J. Percy Adams with the School of American Archaeology made a fine miniature model of Pecos "in later time," and again it was just too much history to lay its ghost to rest. Built in the 16th century, the huge adobe ruin of the Mission stands in silent tribute to the Franciscan padres and their teachings. Abandoned by its last 17 inhabitants in 1838, when they joined their kinsmen at Jemez they made a precious gift of their patron saint, "The Lady of the Angels," to the people of Pecos Village where each year it is remembered with a celebration.

I started and went back and forth on my motorcycle. From the time the first homesteaders and squatters settled down the Pecos River, they pilfered timber for housing, sheds and corrals from the Pecos Mission. Its walls were rapidly crumbling and I put in concrete to slant it up and stabilize it. It looked good but sad to relate, a fellow named Whitkind went over in 1940 and tore out most of it.. But I found those outstanding remnants of viga and corbel and the colors that made the work there worth my time.

W. Templeton Johnson (architect from San Diego, an expert on California mission construction) came over and we divised a little frame, stretching burlap over it, keeping it moist and in shadow and we were able to make scale drawings of all the corbels plus their bed-molds as we found the small sections, for no sooner were they exposed than they went to pieces and we had to work fast.

Some original color could still be seen and with this advantage, I was proud to have the design and color. I believe it was at this point that I began to think that if an Art Museum became a reality and they still wanted me, this type of mission interior of viga-corbel design, would be supremely fitting and beautiful.

A.V. Kidder, with whom I had contacts in the past (See: Nusbaum, Jesse L. *A Basketmaker Cave in Kane County, Utah, with notes on the artifacts by A.V. Kidder and S.J. Guernsey.* New York, 1922, 153 pages),, arrived to make his headquarters at the Valley Ranch. He put up $10 as did I and a few others. J.F. Miller who ran the ranch contributed $250 because of the attraction of visitors and this completed my assignment.

Coronado and the Turk

Rosemary, I roamed the Galisteo basin many times with you and always we talked of the part it played in the Pecos (Cicuye) story (see: Lummis, Charles F. *Pueblo Indian Folk Stories*. Pecos, page 145), of which we know so little. Every time we visited the ruins of San Cristobal, which lies about half way between the Pecos and Jemez Pueblos, with which the old Pecos people were intertwined. And I think of Estevan, the negro, and his story in relation to the Pueblos for he was a member of what we know as an early bit of history in this respect. He was shipwrecked on the coast of Florida in 1528 under a leader, one Panfilo de Narvaez. The majority had lost their lives but there was another survivor, Cabeza de Vaca, and accompanied by this negro Estevan and two other Spaniards, Dorantes and Castillo Maldonado, they succeeded after eight years of great hardship in making their way westward on foot, from tribe to tribe picking up much of the language of the native peoples as they went.

They crossed southern Texas and finally reached the Spanish settlements on the Pacific coast of Mexico. During his wanderings, de Vaca had heard stories of large opulent cities in the north. To New Spain's competent and well-loved Spanish Viceroy, Don Antonio de Mendoza, the stories of Cabeza de Vaca's narritives were good indeed (see: Hammond, George P. *Coronado's Seven Cities*), so much so that he sent out a Franciscan monk, Fray Marcos de Niza, to investigate.

Marcos de Niza, who had just come from Peru and Central America, both recently conquered, was picked to lead the exploring party. With the negro slave Estevan, whom he had bought from Dorantes, and some Mexican Indians he set off for the mysterious country in the Spring of 1539. On the way he was temporarily delayed and Estevan, sent ahead to reconnoiter, exceeded his instructions and pushed through to what is now New Mexico and reached the first of the "Cities." Just what occurred there will never be known, but Estevan was doubtless overbearing and arrogant. History has it he behaved in a manner distinctly distasteful to his native hosts, which reached a climax at Cibola.

A faculty for attracting pretty women did not add to his popularity. He bedecked himself in bright robes, tufts of parrot feathers, bells and gaudy bracelets on his arms and legs. The negro carried with him a magic "gourd" filled with pebbles and decorated with a red and white feather which he would send ahead by a runner to notify the villages of his coming which earned him many gifts of turquoise and skins.

It worked until he reached Hawikuh, the Zuni Pueblo in western New Mexico (see: Hodge, F.W. *The Six Cities of Cibola, 1581-1680*). A Zuni legend today told to the Pueblo's children describes Estevan's violent end: "It is to be believed that a long time ago, when roofs lay over the walls of Kya-ki-me (Hawikuh), when smoke hung over the house tops, and the ladder-rounds were still unbroken (when the pueblo was inhabited), then the Black Mexicans came from their adobes in Everlasting Summerland (Mexico)...then and thus was killed by our Ancients, right where the stone stands down by the arroyo of Kya-ki-me, one of the Black Mexicans (Estevan), a large man with chili lips...Then the rest ran away, chased by our grandfathers and went back toward their country in the land of Everlasting Summer." (See: Kidder, A.V. *The History of Pecos*. Papers of the Southwestern Expedition, 1924). In any event he was promptly killed.

When Niza, following a few days' journey behind, arrived in the area, he was met by some of the survivors of Estevan's Indian escort fleeing southward and was told of the negro's death. Not daring to enter the country openly, yet hesitating to return without some definite information, the Friar ventured to the edge of the valley in which the "Cities" lay, and obtained a view of one of them from a long distance off. He was impressed by its apparent size and by the tales of gold and riches which Estevan's Indians told him. When he had succeeded at last in making his way back to Mexico, he set the Capital on fire with glowing accounts of the wealth of the Seven Cities of Cibola. (See: Bandelier, Adolph. *Niza's Journey.* 1890, Chapter IV.) Perhaps the sun shining on the houses laced with mica made them glitter like gold; perhaps the heat waves rising from the desert in a glorious mirage magnified the size of the town: that it was bigger than two Sevilles...the house walls of solid gold...there were game and wild cattle.

It must be remembered that at this time the Spanish in Mexico were in just the right state of mind to be inflamed by stories of golden lands. The glories of the Montezumas were fresh in everyone's memories and Pizarro had recently dazzled the world with his discovery of the riches of the Incas. Only too willing to believe in the wonders in the north and wishing to profit by them at once, Mendoza immediately equipped a large expedition, placing it under the command of Francisco Vasquez de Coronado and in the Spring 1540 dispatched it upon its journey of discovery and conquest. (See: Winship. *The Coronado Expedition: 1540.* Washington: 1896, page 558.)

When the Coronado expedition came with its big group of soldiers and slaves who were with him at Hawikuh (which I knew well as I had spent three years excavating the Mission there), the people fled and got out of there. He then continued on to Acoma, high up on the rocks and hard to get at. 'Tho they were unfriendly, he remained encamped there for a short time, then pushed on to the Rio Grande, opposite the little town of Bernalillo where they remained for the Winter of 1540, on the west side of the river called the Province of Tiguex. (See: Jones, Paul A. *Quivira*. Second Addendum, pages 42, 43, 135.)

His men apparently began taking advantage of the Indians: they ravished the women and forced them to furnish the keep for all his expedition for that entire Winter, depleting the stores of food the Indians were saving for themselves. Feelings were very high on his departure for the east to Pecos Pueblo where he remained for the Winter of 1541. He soon realized that Pecos was a very strong pueblo — a great force, as others had joined them from Jemez and other villages. It was estimated that there were at least 2,500 people at that time.

Among the newcomers was a man of some mystery, with whom some of Coronado's men had previously met up while encamped at Tiguez, said to have come from Pecos to the East. The Conquistadores called him "the Turk" because he looked like one, wearing his hair bound up in turban style. He was a tall, well-built young fellow of fine physique. This fellow came to the General and told him he had come in response to a notice which had been given to offer themselves as friends: they brought gifts of tanned hides, shields and headpieces, which were gladly received and in return the General gave them some glass dishes, a number of pearls and small bells which they prized highly, as they were things the Indians had never seen.

Coronado had not found the great caches of gold and turquoise they were seeking from the Gran Quivira. Only later did he find out the Indians were decoying and misleading him. The Turk cleverly told Coronado's people with sweet words of gold on the horizon that he knew exactly where Quivira was and persuaded them to let him guide them to it. Sensing the opposition and growing strength at Pecos, Coronado's army got out of there, moving east through the buffalo plains of Texas and Oklahoma, clear to the present town of Lyons, Scotts County, Kansas, to a small place which the Turk said was Quivira.

They found people living in log houses, partly set underground in round rows and they had many buffalo hides, corn and fruits, so they were doing pretty well. But Coronado didn't find what he was looking for although the Turk continued to declare that all was as he said; he was certain now that Turk had been lying, undoubtedly prompted by the people of Pecos. The Turk admitted as much just before he was garroted by the exasperated Spaniards, saying that the people of Pecos wanted them led into the plains until their provisions gave out and they became easy prey for the kill if they returned. In great sorrow Coronado's expedition started now to retrace its way southward, once again to Mexico, demoralized and with few supplies.

As late as 1971, Dr. Waldo Wedel, a very competent archaeologist (from the Smithsonian Institution, Washington, D.C.), while excavating at Quivira, near Lyons, Kansas, found remnants of chained-armor, swords and saddle trappings. Technical analysis has confirmed that these, some of which can be seen in the Courthouse at Lyons, were last used during the time of Coronado's visit.

The Legend of the Pioneer Mother

When you came to live in Santa Fe in 1932, Rosemary, the Ancient City was buzzing with a recent triumph that the then local artists and writers had achieved to keep the Plaza a serene and uncluttered area, by refusing to permit a sculpture of a Pioneer Mother to be placed in the square. The Palace of the Governors loomed imposingly along the length of its north side and a strong sense of the meaning of history was to retain a dignity of simplicity.

Our friends met on the Plaza for morning coffee at cafes like the Mayflower, Faith, Plaza or Gus Mitchell's at Water and Don Gaspar Streets. George King's was the colorful cafe and bar where we took visitors for a bit more of Santa Fe's flavor. The owners, all friends, often joined in a little time-of-day banter. The Hotel La Fonda, under the Harvey Co., was a place of international spirit and much élan. Its gift shop was a place of fascination with glamour from foreign lands, under Herman Schweizer, with whom I had set up the famous Indian room at the Alvarado in Albuquerque in 1916. Here could be seen the poetic fire in the animated oils of artist Paul Lantz and everyone felt the allure of the gently painted murals of artist Olive Rush, that graced the walls and pillars in the New Mexican room.

During New Deal days while I was Director of the Laboratory of Anthropology, I also had a small part in the management of the local chapter of the Arts Commission. Following the stock market crash of 1929, the economic situation was very pressing for all, but especially the artists were suffering. Preliminary to New Deal time a Commission was set up in Washington to assist artists and it was decided that sculptures be included. Joe Davidson, a well-known and fine sculptor was commissioned to sculpt a larger than life size version of a Pioneer Mother. Several copies were to be placed along the old Santa Fe Trail, at the discretion of the Washington Commission and Santa Fe was designated to be one of them.

When Santa Fe people heard of this intrusion of sculptures in the Plaza a great controversy raged. Headed by artists John Sloan and his wife Dolly, there were Willard Nash, Will Shuster, writer Mary Austin and others, who decided that the intrusion was unfitting. Letters and wires grew heated between the local art colony and the Commission in Washington, but decisions had been made far away and there was insistence that Santa Fe was a proper place.

Well, the day came for the sculpture to appear and indeed that afternoon the Pioneer Mother arrived at the corner of Shelby and San Francisco Streets on the Plaza by truck, all swathed in wrappings and accompanied by three men — one, a short fellow named Harry Truman, then working for the Penderghast bosses of Kansas City, and soon to become Vice President of these United States under Franklin Roosevelt. As the truck came to a stop, the Santa Fe group there to meet it immediately expressed refusal and loudly ordered the truck to move on. Someone shouted that life was not lived merely consisting of breathing but in acting and the controversy raged loud and heated, as the Pioneer Mother was unwrapped by the equally determined men on the truck.

When an attempt was made to move the sculpture, Mary Austin, known to all of us as a lady of great literary brilliance and independence, and a formidable and large lady of stature, stepped forward and with no offense to modesty began to kick Harry Truman on the shins.

The Pioneer Mother never left the truck. She was hastily rewrapped and taken to grace the little park on Fourth Street in Albuquerque.

Editor's Note: I went to visit her after hearing this story at first opportunity. I found her beautiful in bonnet and full skirted garment of the day, holding a small child on one arm while another clings to her skirt...truly a madonna of the trail. The story haunted me the Summer of 1978 when Albuquerque sought a "time capsule," and I wondered what it might contain if found in the future. But the Pioneer Mother fittingly graces the area of the old "trail to El Paso del Norte" — a moving and lovely sculpture of Pioneer American Womanhood.
Rosemary Nusbaum.

Art Museum

Shortly after my assignment ended at Pecos, New Mexico, I was assured that the proposed Art Museum was substantially to be constructed according to the architectural plans being prepared by I.H. & W.M. Rapp, architects, subject to such minor changes as may be made from time to time, with the approval of the Director or the building committee and that construction should be done under my continued assignment as Superintendent of Construction for the Museum of New Mexico.

Accompanied by Paul A.F. Walter, executive secretary for the School of American Archaeology, I made a reconnaissance of mission churches and ruins of the Saline Pueblos, often called the "cities that died of fear" (namely, Abo, Tenabo, Chilili, Tajique, Manzano and others), in Torrance and Bernalillo counties. Following this, Templeton Johnson, an expert on the mission architecture of California, accompanied me on a similar reconnaissance of mission churches and ruins in Rio Arriba, Santa Fe, Valencia, Bernalillo, Sandoval, McKinley, San Miguel, Guadalupe and Taos counties.

In contributing the land for the site, Frank Springer did not disclose on April 12, 1916 who was associated with him in providing the $30,000 gift, which was then progressively matched by the State and on April 17 I began the work of clearing the ground for the new structure.

I liked the New Mexico Mission style: the Palace Avenue side predominantly reminiscent of the Acoma Mission, and the Lincoln Avenue side being old Cochiti and Laguna. So we had two attractive fronts with the Palace Avenue side somewhat longer (by 157 feet) and 30 feet wider (being 118 feet deep)than the New Mexico Building at the San Diego Exposition.

I had the plan in my own mind, as the result of long research and work on my desire to create the auditorium and entrance hall to hold to what I had found at Pecos, as infinitely fitting this structure. The barracks building of adobes and wood was still standing when I came to Santa Fe. It extended to the now Bishop Building and at that west end, the army bakery had a small section of space. The north part of the barracks structure ended at what became the Director's residence.

Colonel Jose D. Sena was then head of the school board and vehemently objected to our program and spending this money. He gave Frank Springer a bad time, but it was compromised when we offered — and did turn over to his discretion all lumber and salvage materials as we removed them. (*The New Mexican:* Santa Fe, April 27, 1916: "Some fifty pounds of pieces of Indian pottery, one pot almost complete, with curious pieces of glass and Spanish crockery were were unearthed this morning under direction of Jesse Nusbaum to excavate the foundation for the new Museum at the site of the destroyed Old Barracks. The relics are being carefully cleaned and saved. It is believed this is the site of one of several Indian pueblos which once stood where Santa Fe does now.") When I started I began by tearing down this barracks building and as we demolished the old structure all salvage material, at Sena's request, was turned over to Charles Campbell who was in charge over at the Fort Marcy Hospital. The Army hospital then stood on the site now occupied by the abandoned high school building on Marcy Street directly across from the new Federal Post Office.

There was much beautiful, heavy timber which had originally been obtained from the lumber mill up Canyon Road. I found the steel they had used of inferior kind and the tailor-edged roofing they had initially put on this poor quality building. Since the Government had owned this structure and it was now in the process of being turned over to the School of American Research by the legislature, Colonel Sena had a point.

Almost at once my own problems kept me occupied. Just where the east wall of the auditorium ran, I knew that for a long time this part had been used for privys and the problem of human waste we were confronted with was some seven feet deep. I put in a floating foundation, which required the use of steel; then I put in a one foot thick foundation of concrete, requiring three-quarter inch square reinforcing, lengthwise, and one-half inch rods crosswise, every six inches clear through. This wall has never given one bit.

Rapp and Hendricks on architecture, were set on having the structure completely fireproofed and Hewett agreed with them. I wanted some relief for beauty. They began by using no wood, only panels and sheets of concrete going overhead and ignored my demands for viga treatment. I became adamant on my work in the big auditorium, where I carefully planned to follow the detail I had found at the Pecos Mission.

The magnificent large beams with the three rolls on them are exactly the way we found them at Pecos. I did not have enough money to make the color edged, zig-zag line on these and this was left off to my deep regret, but all were hand carved and I also got the beams in the front entrance area, otherwise visitors would have to come into a concrete floor and plastered ceilings.

I continued insistent and carefully followed the Pecos Mission detail, 'tho all the while Hewett opposed me, but I had the good fortune of Frank Springer's approval. I got these large beams through my connection with a salesman named Larrick who worked for the Benson Lumber Company while I was building the "Painted Desert" in San Diego. I had bought many small shiploads of lumber through him for the San Diego project as they came into that port. I got Larrick out here and took him out to San Ildefonso and said, "I've got to have some beams and they must be large — 12 x 14 inches in dimension — and I want the corbels and the whole thing; something that won't split like these I point out to you here at San Ildefonso that are out in the sun and all going to pieces." He replied, "Well, I'll tell ya, we get big floating rafts that we lash together up in the northwest, in the States of Washington and Oregon, on the river there and we bring down as much as five million board feet of lumber in just logs, some up to 180 feet long; we can get you any kind you want."

I asked, "What does the water do?" He said, "That's the secret of it. That water. They are lashed by chains on the rafts and then towed by tug boat. It's the sap that generally produces rapid splitting. When water replaces the sap as they slowly dry there's very little splitting." I gave him my order with price and because of my connection with the Santa Fe Railway, they worked with me to get them almost at once...Larrick "red-balled" it through.

When the car came into Santa Fe — the heaviest load I've ever seen, still dripping salt water and not sap — I had heavy tarps keep them wet to prevent quick drying. A man was killed at Benson Lumber Company doing our work. They had promised to cut the corbels by jigsaw there prior to shipment here, and the operator did not keep the saw well tightened and it threw it right through his body. I had to teach a group of inexperienced workers to handle saws and as we worked a large piece of steel tipped over and came down on the back of my knees — always bothered me afterward. But I had good men like Sam Huddleston and Glen Russell and others.

I already knew where I was going to get the diagonal sapplings I wanted, as I had been up into the Sangre de Cristo Mountains many times on my motor-cycle and I knew where they were. You see the results of the forest fire up there from Santa Fe very clearly, which took place in early army days in the Horses-head Basin. I'd examined the quaking aspen that had fallen in that fire, many on top of one another. Those standing upright were grey in color but still in good firm condition because they were held off the ground. Those that had fallen, rot-ted. Many that stayed off the ground were generally fine with the good color characteristics I was looking for so I had a local workman named Beatrice Vigil, go up there with his team and wagon and kept him going back and forth for quite some time. He became proficient at picking just the dry ones and brought them down. Again I selected and we made them go twice as far by choosing the nice ones and splitting them, keeping the round grey edge down. Hewett said very little through this period but the men thought he bore some envy.

THE WOMEN'S BOARD ROOM: It had been planned that the women's board room be on the second floor. When we got to this room, I thought it should be something other than just plain concrete slabs, one reason being the importance that Hewett always placed on the woman's board. The ladies always carried the torch and worked on their husbands to keep them in line and he won many of his desires that way. I worked out a very fine design for an elaborate ceiling, vigas, carving, color, the whole thing...even designed and made some furniture. Hewett was gone while I was doing this and Frank Springer and the other men approved. The upshot of it was when Hewett returned, he hit the ceiling. I'd not seen him angrier. I was sure I'd be fired right there but he couldn't get rid of me. Finally he decided he would ask the women what could be done to harmonize the ceiling, for the entire room was completed. In the carving, I'd used burnt orange in the grooves and two shades of blue to work out the pattern. It was stunning. But Hewett had the ladies bring all the things they should have. One lady brought a paisley embroidered shawl with all the colors of the rainbow. Others brought samples of their wishes. Nothing seemed suitable.

Robert Henri, a famous artist then painting in Taos, came down to make some tests. He worked from the first morning light until dusk on the color change. Finally he told Hewett, "I cannot improve on what Jess has done. What you can do is bring the colors down into the curtains and the seats about the room and that will tie it in if you wish this." It was Robert Henri who won this case for me and this has been a famous room ever since. It has never been changed.

In the meantime Frank Springer, with the foresight and generosity he had shown throughout, had secured title to the building on the north for about $10,000. It had been an official residence of Fort Marcy and he asked me to transform it into a typical "New Mexico style" dwelling, compatible with the Art Museum architecture and of practical utility as a residence for the Director. While waiting for a delayed shipment of steel I completed this conforming project and it brought us the ten feet additional width we needed; as otherwise the Art Museum would have been too tight to the street.

Interesting and still existing are the murals in the auditorium. One of the Springer daughters, Eva, was a talented artist working in miniatures and while studying in Paris she became interested in the work of a young artist Donald Beauregard. She succeeded in interesting her father in the young man's work and Springer bought a number of his paintings. These hung in the upstairs gallery for years. Springer put him in charge of the mural decorations for the school. Then he decided to put the story of St. Francis into murals as a tribute to the auditorium which he named after his favorite Saint and to mount them in panels therein. Beauregard made sketches suggestive of the convent and monastery at La Rabida, near Palos, the little port from whence Columbus had set sail for the New World. He had completed and placed part of them when he died suddenly April 30, 1941. Artists Carlos Vierra and Kenneth M. Chapman then completed his assignment.

Today the symmetry of the auditorium has been ruined by the addition of the pipe organ and the grill is so bad. It ran the platform clear out and changed the entire aspect. I had put in hidden lights to reflect on the ceiling downward. The original concept I fought for was the form of a cross with transept and nave. The organ fills one arm of the cross and, to my regret, spoils the whole thing.

Governor Lew Wallace

Interior Room, Palace of the Governors, before restoration, 1909.

San Ildefonso Indian next to puddled adobe brick wall, Palace of the Governors, Santa Fe, at the time of restoration. Photo by Jesse Nusbaum, 1910.

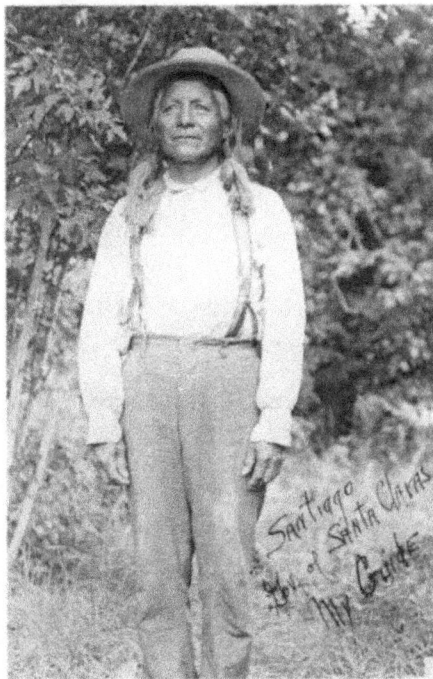

Santiago Naranjo, 5-time Governor of Santa Clara Pueblo, 1909. Photo by Jesse Nusbaum

"I wanted my great friend to see Mesa Verde, because he said he would like to. He always said, "Well, I can't go. I have to look after my people.""

Jesse Nusbaum

Santiago Naranjo at ruin of Tsankawi with Jesse Nusbaum who took the photo.

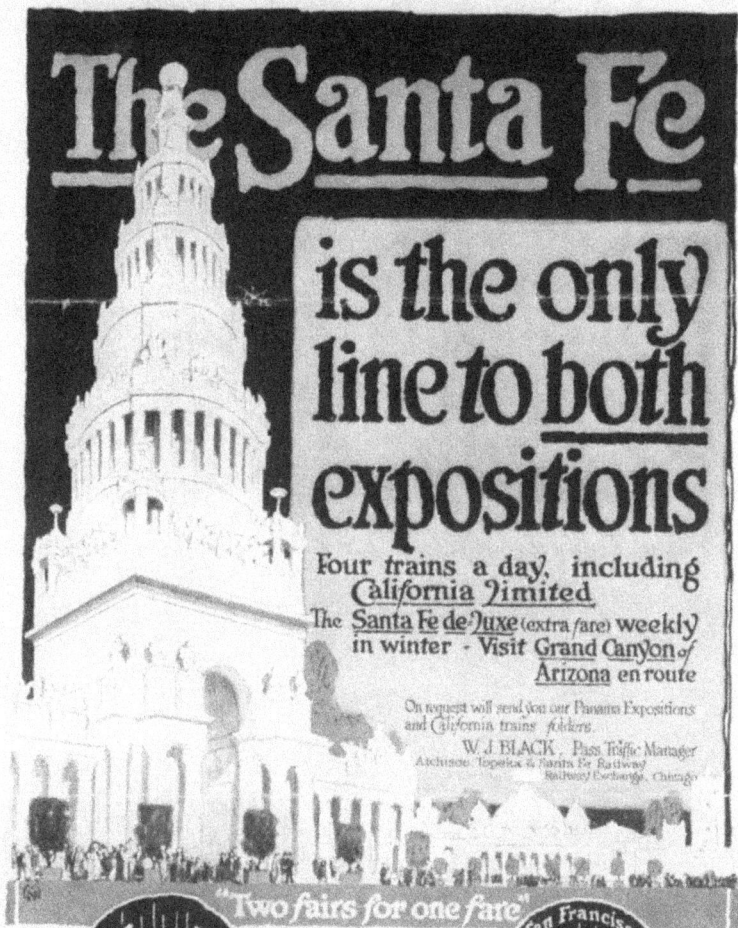

Santa Fe Railroad promotional cover to San Diego Exposition, 1915.

Making pottery at the Painted Desert Exhibit, San Diego, 1915.
San Ildefonso potters, Nacamina & Maria Martinez, at work. Photo by Jesse Nusbaum.

The Zuni Pueblo section of Painted Desert Exhibit, San Diego Exposition. 1915. Photo by Jesse Nusbaum.

Pecos Mission, 1915, after basal wall stabilization. Photo by Jesse Nusbaum.

The ruins of the old Pecos Mission, on side of ruined Pecos Pueblo, near Santa Fe, New Mexico.

"...it was just too much history to lay its ghost to rest... the huge adobe ruin...stands in silent tribute to the Franciscan Padres and their teachings."

Jesse Nusbaum

Art Museum near completion, Santa Fe, 1917. Photo by Jesse Nusbaum

In front of Art Museum, 1917. Mr. Harmon Hendricks (left), Mr. & Mrs. Goerge Heye. Photo by Jesse Nusbaum

Chapman Ballard.
Photo courtesy Kit Carson Memorial Foundation, Inc.

Ouray Ute War Chief, Shavano.
Photo courtesy Denver Public Library Western Collection.

Jesse L. Nusbaum at Cliff Palace, 1944

Leader of the Southern Utes, "Buckskin Charlie."

Jesse Nusbaum at work bracing 2-story tower Balcony House, Mesa Verde, 1910. Photo by Jesse Nusbaum.

Jesse Nusbaum with camera, Alfred Kidder with canteen. Reconnaissance at Mesa Verde, 1908. Photo by Jesse Nusbaum

Taking off for the west side of Mesa Verde. Left to right: "Coots" Frink, Alfred V. Kidder, Jesse Nusbaum. Photo by Jesse Nusbaum.

The Princess and Crown Prince Gustav Adolphus of Sweden at Cliff Palace, Mesa Verde, while Jesse was Superintendent. Photo by George L. Beam, Denver, Colorado.

"The Pioneer Photographer," Wm. H. Jackson.

Henry F. Morgan at age 91; photo sent to Jesse Nusbaum after their meeting.

Cliff Palace, Mesa Verde. Left to right: John D. Rockefeller, Jr., Bert Mattison and Dr. R.W. Corwin. Photo by Jesse Nusbaum reproduced courtesy Denver Public Library Western Collection.

Horizontal view, east half, Cliff Palace

Survey of Colorado, 1873

Hayden
Stevenson
Holman
Jones

W.H. Holmes
W. D. Whitney
Gardner

...the final Act provided that
"the Mesa Verde National Park is created,
a protective custody over all ruins within
five miles to its exterior limits."

Part IV: THE OLD TIME

THE FOLLOWING ARTICLE IS REPRINTED IN ITS ENTIRETY FROM:
The Daily News, September 20, 1901, Denver, Colorado.
"SCIENTISTS VISIT CLIFF PALACE"
By Helen M. Ring (a member of the party)

A party consisting of Mrs. Gilbert McClurg of Colorado Springs; Dr. and Mrs. J.W. Fewkes, of Washington; Dr. G.G. McCurdy, of Yale University Museum; Mrs. W.S. Peabody; Mrs. J.D. Whitmore; Mrs. J.L. McNeil; Dr. Frank Russell of the B.A.E. and Mrs. Russell; Prof. H.B. Ward of the Unviersity of Nebraska; Prof. Nutting of Iowa University; Mr. Frank Hitchcock; Prof. A.B. Lewis of the University of Nebraska; Prof. U.S. Weatherly of Indiana State University; Miss Putnam of Davenport, Iowa; Miss Helen M. Ring of Providence, R.I. and Miss Sutherland of Pittsburgh.

The party drove by wagon down the Mancos Canyon on Thursday, September 5, 1901 as far as the wagon road went, which was about two miles east of the mouth of Cliff Canyon [present Soda].

At the termination of the road, the party, the largest that ever visited the cliffs, camped for the night, the place being named, out of respect for the distinguished visitors, 'Camp Science.'

The journey was continued next morning with saddle horses and the difficult ascent of the Cliff Palace was made by all but a few of the visitors. On the way Dr. Fewkes was invited to name a most interesting ruin, till then nameless. It consists of two houses, placed one above the other, with a narrow shelf of rocks between, high in the left side of Cliff Canyon and is in an excellent state of preservation.

The learned Doctor decided it should be called Hemenway House, in honor of the late Mrs. Mary Hemenway of Boston. The choice seemed to all an especially happy one, as it is certainly appropriate that one of the ruins, whose preservation is the chosen work of an association of Colorado Women, should bear a name of a woman who rendered such great service to the cause of archaeological investigations in the Southwest."

From three or four news clippings about this trip we knew the party left Mancos in four camp wagons accompanied by a mess wagon and saddle horses. After camping the night, they rode by horseback the next day straight to Cliff Palace, leaving the horses when the going got too rough and proceeded on foot. As they did not have time to go to more ruins than Cliff Palace, some of the party on returning to the Mancos Canyon camp that night wanted Al Wetherill (brother of Richard Wetherill) to guide them back the next day to Spruce Tree Ruin. C.B. Kelly (Kelly, from Mancos, served as Jesse Nusbaum's guide and pack and saddle animal operator in 1907 and 1908, and again in 1910 when Nusbaum excavated and stabilized the ruin of Balcony House at Mesa Verde).

Early Visits to the Mesa Verde

From time to time over a long period, I always visited with Francis Cheetham, attorney and local historian, whenever I chanced to be in the vicinity of Taos, New Mexico. In the mid 1930s, when we were talking about the many years I spent in Mesa Verde as Superintendent and Archaeologist, I chanced to mention the long-publicized claim of Richard Wetherill and Charles Mason that they discovered Cliff Palace in late December 1888.

Cheetham said that Chapman Ballard, cherished friend and long-time local rancher was mad as hell about this Wetherill claim and said he would refute this and write the true story about its discovery when he was on the 1875 Survey of the North Boundary of the Southern Ute Reservation, and "get with it right away." When I next saw Cheetham, he told me Ballard had died suddenly — that he had never reviewed a single portion of such a report.

A lady, long interested in Mesa Verde, and a former resident of Colorado Springs, in writing me for certain information on Nordenskiöld's Mesa Verde excavations of 1891, first cited for me the long-sought and refuting true story of the 1875 discovery of Cliff Palace by Chapman Ballard, which follows:

"CHAPMAN BALLARD OF TAOS, VISITS HERE.
ONE OF FIRST TO SEE MESA VERDE RUINS.
Colorado Springs Gazette, October 20, 1937, p. 8

History is wrong in attributing the discovery of the Mesa Verde cliff dwellings to the Wetherald [sic: Wetherill] brothers in 1880 [1888], Chapman Ballard of Taos, New Mexico, who is visiting friends here, declares.

Ballard who is 83 years old, took occasion while visiting Mr. and Mrs. John C. Hershey, 3612 West Colorado Avenue, to refute the Wetherill claim. He says that he was one of a party of surveyors who saw the Cliff Palace and other ruins on the Mesa Verde in the Summer of 1875.

There was no excitement in the park when, as a guide related that the ruins were discovered by the Wetherills, Mr. Ballard corrected him saying that he and others of a party of government surveyors had seen them long before. He was told every effort would be made to unearth the report of the survey to see if the engineer in charge had so recorded it at the time. He was asked much about the survey, which proved a thrilling story of Indian opposition, and finally cooperation, and he told it over last week in Colorado Springs, where he expects to remain for some time, visiting other old haunts with the Hershey's.

Mr. Ballard says he came west from Missouri and rode a long distance to enlist at Fort Garland in the San Luis Valley, but when he got in sight of the flag at the fort he changed his mind. He says it was lucky for him he did so, for if he had not, the Seventh regiment being encamped there, he would probably have died with the others who were massacred with Custer.

But as to the Mesa Verde. Mr. Ballard was with two others who were looking for places to settle. They went into New Mexico and he joined the surveying party. The government then did its surveying in the west, he says by contract. The contractor's name was Darling and a brother of his accompanied the party as guide and interpreter, as the Indians spoke more or less Spanish, but no English. The engineer's name he says was James Miller. They set out for Conejos, which was near where the town of Antonito now is, in the southern part of Colorado.

'It was while we were running the north line of the South Ute Reservation that we saw the Mesa Verde ruin.' he says. 'There were ten or eleven of us in the party. I think it must have been in July. I do not remember which one of the party saw the Cliff Palace first, but it could be seen plainly from where we were working. We were on the opposite side of the canyon, but we all went to it at once and inspected it and other ruins, seeing much broken pottery about. Of course, much that can be seen now in the Mesa Verde national park had not then been uncovered. The discovery created much interest among us. Whether it was mentioned in the report of the survey I don't know.'

WAS FIRST RETURN VISIT TO RUINS

Mr. Ballard has been a pioneer visitor in many parts of the State and New Mexico and has long ranched near Taos, but said he had never gone to the Mesa Verde ruins since seeing them in what he believes to have been the first sight of them by white men, tho he had had a number of invitations to go, until he went with the Hershey's.

'Did you have any trouble with Indians when making the survey?' he was asked.

'Oh, a little,' he said. 'One day as we were moving along we found ourselves stopped by about thirty Indians lined up right in front of us, with guns across their saddles. They asked us what we were doing.

'We told them we were making pictures. They asked to see the pictures. Of course, we had none so then we told them what we were engaged in. They seemed to understand all about it and pointing to a distant range of mountains, told us we could go over there and run our line, but not where we were working.

'Some of the men said they were engaged to survey but not to fight Indians. So we turned back to Pagosa Springs [Old Fort Lewis military reservation], where the hot springs were just as they are today. We waited about thirty days while the matter of the survey was taken up with Chief Ouray, and then he sent his War Chief, Shavano to remain with us to see we were not attacked. When we went back to work the whole valley was filled with tepees. There must have been several hundred Indians about. But they did not interfere with us as we continued to run the line.'

We had some triangulations to make that took us far from the camp and twice were three days and nights without water. Jim Miller, the engineer, could not stand this as well as others and at times their tongues swelled up until it was like a cucumber. Several times we dug for water and on occasions had to wait for it to drip out of a bank while we were nearly dead of thirst.'

Mr. Ballard told us how the surveyors when in different groups would signal to each other with smudges, and of how sometimes they would see no answering smudge and realize they were lost. He said they had about twenty five pack animals on which to move their equipment as there were no roads in any of the part of the country where they were working.

He was in Cripple Creek in early days of the gold excitement and also in Aspen and other mining camps, in early days. For a while he was engaged in freighting. His visit to Mesa Verde national park he says has vividly brought back to him his old adventures while with the government survey party."

As a matter of record, Rosemary, we now know that Chapman Ballard, Frank Morgan, Dr. William Robert Winters, James Frink and S.E. Osborn progressively discovered and inspected this largest Cliff dwelling (Cliff Palace) among others during the period 1875 to 1885.

The Mesa Verde

Prior to 1907, by assignment of the Secretary of the Smithsonian, Dr. Edgar L. Hewett served for nearly a decade in Washington as secretary and liaison agent with interested members of Congress for the many scientific associations, museums and archaeological societies which had been striving for years and years to achieve, through congressional legislation, an Act for the preservation of American antiquities. To preserve those on public domain from disturbance, damaging, destruction and loss due to unscientific methods then rampant, and for like objectives and public benefits, for an Act to enjoin for the establishment of the Mesa Verde National Park.

Both Acts were finally passed by Congress and signed by the President in 1906. With respect to the last Act: due to the adamant opposition of the Southern Ute Indians to exchange any of the Reservation lands — on which most of the largest and most notable and best known cliff dwellings were located — for other lands of their selection, the final Act provided that "the Mesa Verde National Park is created, a protective custody over all ruins within five miles to its exterior limits."

Early in 1907, in preparation for such exchange of lands, the Secretary of the Interior who also had jurisdiction over the Southern Utes, asked Dr. Hewett to undertake an archaeological survey of all ruins on Reservation lands essential to the Park's dominion and to determine the related boundaries thereof. He was to make specific recommendations as to both features and in his contracts to furnish specific comprehensive photographs of all notable ruins and their canyon and mesa environs, which the Department needed to determine the minimum acreage of Reservations lands essential to the enlargement of the Park.

After recruiting five members from his Summer expedition at Harvard University, he consulted with Dr. Snyder, President of what was then called Colorado State Normal University at Greeley (now Colorado State Teachers College), under whom he had previously served, telling him of his great need during the ensuing summer for his Mesa Verde expedition of a young and agile man, skilled in photography and interested in archaeology. Snyder recommended me at once, and Dr. Hewett whom I had known for several years, immediately contracted to furnish transportation, subsistence and photographic supplies, plus $50 to me for my summer's work...provided I would furnish at my own expense a 5 x 7 View Camera equipped with regular, wide-angle and telephoto lenses — Zeiss or equal — and all other necessary photographic equipment including, if possible, a 6-power binocular to facilitate ruin locations. Said equipment cost me approximately $215.

I met Hewett, archaeologists A.V. Kidder and S.G. Morley, and the other members from Harvard at the Mancos railhead. Charley Kelly packed us in with our food and supplies, etc., over the Mancos and Frink Trails to his 2-room, cedar log cabin with roofed shelter between the rooms, on the rimrock at the head of Spruce Tree Canyon, just west of the location where, in 1908 Phil Bauer built the stock watering reservoir for Major Hans Randolph, the first appointed Superinten- dent. Hewett left us in about ten days and thereafter Ted Kidder became my primary associate, sharing with me in packing — on back and in hand — all the photographic equipment, rope and other materials for use on our daily hikes across mesa and canyon terrain from the camping base, in order to make as com- plete a photographic and location record as Hewett desired of the ruins on the Ute Reservation that should be embraced within the National Park area.

Hewett was much pleased with my comprehensive photographic report. Based primarily on his report to the Secretary of the Interior, his representations and negotiations with the Winnemuchi band of Utes, they agreed to exchange 19,250 acres of other federal lands west of the Park for the 12,760 acres of Ute reservation that were needed to bring the major cliff dwellings of the Mesa Verde under domination of the Mesa Verde National Park. This exchange agree- ment was signed May 10, 1911, though it was not approved by Congress until 1913, so the area was not added until then.

In the late Summer of 1908, Kidder and I were returned to Mesa Verde to complete photography of the important Wetherill cliff dwellings on Wetherill mesa and the westernmost section of the Park. Our other assignments were in the McElmo canyon and the Hovenweep canyon area for me. I followed my basic assignment of making a comprehensive record via horseback of all the notable ruins in the Hovenweep region including McElmo, Yellowjacket and related branches thereof — and of all phases of S.G. Morley's excavation of the South House of Cannon Ball Ruin, located about two miles northeasterly of Jim Holly's ranch on the north rim of Home Mesa overlooking Yellowjacket or Hovenweep canyons — and serve as business manager of the dig on which Morley was assisted by five Harvard students — Then, on Hewett's return, saddle-back with him about 45 miles northwest to Byron Cumming's first ar- chaeological dig on Alkali Ridge, Utah, where Ted Kidder was serving, per Hewett's arrangements, as dig foreman — and finally, on completion of Cannon Ball and Alkali Ridge digs, return to Mesa Verde with Kidder to complete the recordings of Wetherill Mesa cliff dwellings. After that I was to go with Kidder, Morley and his crew to join Hewett for brief preliminary excavations within main Frijoles or present Bandelier National Monument.

In the early Fall of 1910, pursuant to the recommendations of Smith- sonian, Hewett again returned me to Mesa Verde to clean up the debris of past pot-hunting, plus repair and firmly stabilize the badly cracked and failing walls of Balcony House cliff dwelling. The Colorado Cliff Dwellers Association con- tributed $1,000 toward this project; the D&RG Railroad agreed to provide passes for skilled men who would be needed. I recruited a good stone mason, and an engineer at Greeley, Colorado, and persuaded my father, a thoroughly competent building contractor to assist me, recruiting the balance of needed labor at Mancos, Colorado. Once again Charley Kelly was enlisted to pack our expedition to the frame shack that Fewkes used the previous Summer on his Cliff Palace project...situated directly on the rim over this cliff dwelling. Hewett accompanied us, remained one day, then returned with Kelly to Mancos after he had agreed to my program of work on Balcony House.

With the assistance of my able crew the badly cracked and failing walls of Balcony House cliff dwelling were slowly closed by the process of dampening the open cracks of free-standing walls and by anchoring to the rear cave walls by means of steel rods, turn buckles and vertical angle-rod braces, thus insuring the fronting walls up to more than two stories in height against crashing to the top of the talus slope 20 feet or more below as other walls had. Not once since 1910, to the present time has there been need for adjusting a single part of the harness, or other bracings we put in to hold these walls.

The Balcony House project had required ten weeks of dedicated work. Due to abnormally heavy snowfall, the others had already left and J. Percy Adams agreed to await the arrival of Hewett with me. He had instructed me to remain there, as he wanted to inspect the completed work before I departed. Adams and I eagerly awaited his arrival with Dr. Patton of the Archaeological Institute in Connecticut, for we were painfully near the end of our food supply.

They finally arrived with Charley Kelly so late in the afternoon that Jack and I had to build small fires in Balcony House to show them the completed job, as they stated the desire to return the following day to continue their inspection trip. Heavy snowfall started up once again shortly after their departure. Since Kelly had only three saddle horses we could not return to Mancos with them. Kelly was to return for us to pack out our essential impedimenta.

We had exhausted the last remnants of our food supply and the next morning sensing unusual weather, Jack and I left early, burdened with camera and other essential equipment to hike to Cortez over the north rim. By dusk, after breaking trail up to waist high snow drifts near the north rim, we started down the Kelly Trail to his pack-cabin or shed at the toe of the Mesa Verde, hoping to spend the balance of the night there.

We found the shack devoid of stove, firewood or food — we were wet, exhausted and it was becoming bitterly cold...and we had to continue to Cortez. By the time we reached the Mancos and Cortez road, it was pitch dark. Cattle had been trailed over it and the gumbo surface was deeply tracked with pot-holes and frozen stiff. The last few miles of hiking in pitch darkness — stumbling over such cut-up gumbo was plain torture for hikers. We finally found shelter and warmth at Cortez well after midnight. Lacking Winter footgear and apparel we would have frozen if we had not kept moving.

After the Park travel season closed at the Mesa Verde, October 15, 1920, the park ranger and his wife who operated the public accomodation concession there opposite Spruce Tree clearing, his father-in-law who was Superintendent and his wife, all moved to Mancos for the winter. Then Steven T. Mather, Director of the National Park Service wired the Superintendent that he was arriving at Mancos with J. Walter Fewkes of the Smithsonian, Rodger Toll of Denver and Frank Wadleigh of the D&RG Railway to make his first inspection of the Mesa Verde with the Superintendent. He ordered immediate arrangements for wagon transportation, food and bedding for his party and to be met on their arrival two days later by narrow gauge at Mancos. The Superintendent wired Mather that the road to Spruce Tree camp was closed by snowfall, that inspection was impossible at this time. Mather wired him to get some more teams of horses, that snowfall would not delay his schedule — and it didn't.

Before their arrival, Dr. Fewkes, who had been seasonally excavating, cleaning up and repairing major cliff dwellings and mesa-top ruins since 1907 through Smithsonian cooperation, had complained bitterly to the National Park Service that the Mesa Verde ranger, with the help of other Park employees, had been excavating and unscientifically looting artifacts from the ruins he planned to excavate and repair the following summer. After his return to Washington, he said that this ranger and his father-in-law, the Superintendent, had insisted that artifacts so collected were their personal — and not Federal — property, therefore, they had the right to exhibit such collection to Park visitors ...in five locked cases installed by the Government in the former ranger's quarters overlooking Spruce Tree house and to hold the keys thereto in their possession. Mather told the Superintendent that general conditions of operation were incredibly bad, the very worst he had ever found in any National Park, and what he must do the following Spring to improve these urgent matters.

In early May 1921, while employed as a staff member of the Museum of the American Indian in New York City, I was informed by an associate F.W. Hodge, previously with the Smithsonian and with whom I had worked in the Southwest as principal assistant on explorations and excavations for some years, that Assistant Director of the National Park Service Cammerer had twice interviewed him concerning my qualifications for appointment to Superintendent of Mesa Verde. Hodge informed him I was anxious to return to the Southwest.

About ten days later I received a letter from the Senior Senator from Colorado, L.C. Phipps, summoning me to his office for a personal hearing on the Park Service's plan to appoint me Superintendent of Mesa Verde. Director Mather and and Assistant Director Cammerer accompanied me to the appointment. Following introduction and preliminary statements, the Senator asked a series of statistical questions and others pertinent to the Mesa Verde, probably obtained by his staff from Park Service and other publications. My answers were prompt, factual and obviously disconcerting to him. Next from a listing obtained from his cronies in Mancos and Cortez, communities nearest the Park where politics were heavy and rough at the time, principally by the Republican chairman of Montezuma County, who was the Indian trader at Towaoc and wanted the appointment himself, he charged that I was a Democrat, not an archaeologist, that I had no experience in administration, none at building or other construction and further was not a resident of Colorado. I had a rebuttal to every charge and he became nervous and distraught. Director Mather then took over and I have never seen him angrier in the many years I knew him. He affirmed that in the future all National Parks would be administered by him in the public's interest and by Superintendents who were eminently qualified for service in the parks and not by politicians. He was so forceful in his arguments that the Senator said he would approve my appointment to a Superintendency in Colorado which he had approved or cleared in advance. Later and despite this ultimatum, Mr. Mather appointed Rodger Toll, Henry Toll's brother who had previously served for a short time, as Superintendent of Rocky Mountain National Park without advance approval of the Senator, who then went all out.

Armed with my appointment as Superintendent to Mesa Verde, I resigned from the Museum and arrived in Mancos in late May. At the Park office I discussed the state of Park affairs with the Superintendent I was replacing, then for the balance of that day and the two following days with his clerk, a man of 70 years, appointed as a ranger, but not serving due to age. Since the Superintendent was not in a position to do other than sign his name to a letter prepared for his signature, I discussed all matters of immediately concern to me. The clerk kept the books on the current status of appropriations and outstanding obligations for the fiscal year, which was about to end June 30th of that year.

The Park entrance was then passable and I phoned the other ranger, the son-in-law of the outgoing Superintendent, to drive to Mancos and take me to the Park. I assumed he would be driving the recently purchased Model T Ford, a four-door enclosed car which I had been informed in Washington, cost $1,300 and would be the official car. I was surprised on his arrival to see he was driving a Model T Ford without a windshield — actually a chassis on which he had mounted a green painted delivery box in the rear and between it and the instrument board had mounted a ranch wagon seat board on which an old automobile cushion was placed. I asked him "how come?" He answered that his father-in-law and some friends had made one trip to the Park in the new closed car and had to push it up most of the grade because it was underpowered, so on their return the closed body had been sold to Haller's garage for $200, the gas tank and instrument-warden switch had gone with the body and as a result he had a local rancher make a new body and had installed a new gas tank, switch and seat thereto and it was the only car available for transporting supplies to his head-quarters in the Park. Before leaving Mancos I informed the clerk I would establish residence in the Park from the time of my arrival at the location of Spruce Tree camp and to arrange for concessioner's accomodations there and that I hoped to start building a Superintendent's residence in the Fall.

Again an uproar ensued. All stated that Superintendents had always resided in Mancos adjacent to the Park office there, that the entrance road would be closed winter-long by deep snow fall. No white person had ever lived atop the Mesa Verde during the long winter period. My initial two hour auto trip as Superintendent from the entrance to the Park to Spruce Tree camp was over the single lane buggy road on which the first Superintendent Hans Randolph had started construction in 1908 and the third fellow, my predecessor had finally opened to horse drawn vehicles in 1914, which road was a major concern to me because of its excessive length. There were grades running up to twenty-thirty percent or more for short stretches and a large number of successively sharp switch backs over which even a Ford had to back and fill even to get around one of them.

What I saw at the end of the road was an unholy mess. There was a grand commingling within a small area overlooking Spruce Tree camp of concessioner's property consisting of kitchen, dining room and related facilities, including two single room framed cabins and seven floor tents. The government property was a log cabin — rangers quarters recently converted to museum pur-poses when a new framed cottage had been built for this purpose — with a most conspicuous automobile shed of rough board, pitched roof construction sup-ported by high poles, barbed wire and odd tools, as well as articles of in-discriminate sorts. What I observed in the next two weeks about this commin-gling situation and what had to be done by the Park Service in the public interest was to establish first, sole and firm control of all activities in the Park, which became my immediate and paramount concern.

The use by the ranger of the Park Ford for transportation concession supplies and for personal purposes was prohibited. I had water piped from the Park storage tank to a roadside faucet for visitors convenience, constructed two "pit" toilets screened by cedar barricades to the rear of the automobile shed, thus ending visitors dependence on two in the concessioner's backyard. Visitor registration was shifted and issuance of Park permits, questions and Park pam-phlets from the concessioner's main building to the Park museum where a ranger or Park relief employee handled these features with greater dispatch and effi-ciency. The practice was terminated whereby the eight-year-old son of the ranger and other boys would jump on the running boards of incoming cars and competitively solicit their services as guides to all the ruins, for a fee, on the premise that they knew all about the Mesa Verde and its archaeology. Morning and afternoon schedules of trips to the ruins were inaugurated, conducted by rangers or other employess I indoctrinated and trained for such service.

By such means ruins were protected from visitors damage, which told a related story of the Mesa Verde. When I went out to look at the ruins I had found kids climbing all over the walls and people climbing and photographing as they wished. They were picking up any and all shards and at that time there were many. I also started a large cedar-crotch pole enclosure adjacent to the museum, dug and rock lined a shallow camp fire pit, and placed long split log benches with back rests around it so that I could begin giving regular evening camp fire talks to visitors, principally on Mesa Verde archaeology and, in context explain the purposes and objectives of the preservation of American antiquities act, the penalties for its violation in Mesa Verde National Park and all other Federal lands.

I constructed a short access loop road, cleared a series of bordering parking, camping spaces and installed two more "pit" toilets at the nearest suitable location apart from the Park's water supply storage tank and piped water was extended with faucets for camping use. The purpose was to terminate random camping in any place that visitors could drive cars off the main entrance road and in the headquarters area due to consequent damaging and loss of natural vegetative cover and the fire hazard.

Reacting to Director Mather's order at his first inspection, the prior Superintendent had had his ranger, in the Spring of 1921, clear a sizeable area on the opposite side of Spruce Tree canyon, more than two miles round trip from the concessioner's nearest faucet, dig two pits and remove every vestige of dry wood fuel for camping purposes. No one to my knowledge ever camped there. Methods had always been directed to force all advantage toward the concession and keep the Park Service clear out of the picture. The political picture was obvious. There was hardly a directional or distance road sign in the Park, so as funds became available, suitable place name signs, enameled and enduring, were placed. Visitors had long complained that Mesa Verde was practically devoid of signs for reasons requiring no explanation. If a fender hopping youngster was not retained as a guide, you did not know where to find or get to a ruin.

Confirmed by evidence, found pertinent to payroll examination, was the fact that the ranger and his helpers had been paid by the Park Service for time devoted to illegally excavating and looting Park ruins of the large collection of artifacts exhibited in the Park museum in the five locked cases, for which the ranger did indeed hold the keys and claim such collections were personal property. Prior to the departure of all concession personnel at the close of the Park travel season October 15, 1921 for Mancos, I conferred with the concessioner who was incapable for reasons of physical and mental debilities from remaining through the Winter. About seven months were spent tending his own business in Mancos and only five months per annum to the Park — most unsatisfactory.

I stated that I would seize the collections as Government property, file Antiquities Act violation charges against him if he failed to turn over to me as Superintendent of Mesa Verde National Park, the collection of artifacts, the keys to the five exhibit cases and submit his resignation as ranger...all of which was promptly done and the atmosphere was cleared so we could get started. I was further convinced that confidential business matters were being disclosed elsewhere. There was only a telephone over which to talk with the clerk in the Park office. Wires coming in to me were phoned out from the station agent at Mancos who received them. Mine were called back in. All information was spreading and when going into Mancos, I found that people knew things that had taken place and it could come over one source only: the phone. I made contact with the Colorado Mountain States manager, Paul A. Holland and asked for a new operator. The operator relieved turned out to be the daughter of the former Superintendent and I was, and had from the first, been working against one family who held key political jobs.

Now I received a call from the Senator from Colorado at the Park. He had been informed by regional cronies that I had established my official residence there, when I so confirmed, he instructed me to return promptly to Mancos, where all previous Superintendents had resided near the Park office. I informed him I would continue to reside in the Park. He then stated: "It's your responsibility to run the Park and attend to Republican lines in that region and let the ranger run the Park." I informed him I would continue to reside in the Park, that I'd pledged to administer the Park in the public interest and I planned to devote full time to this responsibility and finally to terminate the commingling of consession structures and related facilities with those of the Park service.

A loop access road was constructed by the Park Service bordering the sheer wall perimeter, of the promontory between Spruce and Spruce Tree canyons, southward of the concession's main building. After spaces were cleared bordering the road by skids and on beams and dollies, I moved all concession structures to their new locations and the water line was extended to serve this area. Only by such cooperative means could the Park recover space so vacated for planned development as Park headquarters.

After this, things moved along and worth noting is a visit which followed from Senator Rice Means and his wife. After spending days conducting them through the main ruins I asked them to a cool drink on the porch. Almost at once I answered a loud knocking on the rear door, the man and woman standing there introduced themselves as from Denver, he said he was a member of the K.K.K. and his wife head of the Klavern. He further informed me that Senator Means and others from the local town were assembled there by special dispensation and for $25 I would become a Klansman. He stated that after campfire that night they planned a torch light parade around the circle then take me over to Sun

76

Temple and induct me by the light of a burning cross in the ruin. He further stated that I could then always call on local Klansmen for any help if trouble occurred in the Park. I promptly told him I was not interested in his proposal, that the ranger force would handle any matter in the Park, that I opposed both torchlight parade and the use of a ruin for such purpose as they were contemplating. After the Means left I tipped off the sole ranger and half dozen other employees to assemble before the campfire program was over and be prepared to break up any torchlight parade that might develop. A bit later I went up into a near shack and when I lighted a match, I found these employees sitting on the floor with pick handles in hand to stop any possible disturbance.

Another stark fact was that the Mesa Verde had been overgrazed for years. Prior to the establishment of the Park in 1906 and through the time of my third work assignment there in 1907, it was clearly manifest to me on my return a decade later, as Superintendent in 1921, that prodigious overgrazing of range cover, including sagebrush and shrubbery, plus cattle-tramping had reduced the former conditions to a shambles. Although Park grazing permits issued since 1907 never authorized grazing permits over 850 head at $1.25 per head per annum, the owner of the three tracts of patented lands in the Park, totalling 320 acres, including five wells and windmills, completely monopolized the water sources and grazing in the Park. He received the permits but in the absence of ranger checks, grazing far more than permitted, up to a maximum of 4,800 instead of the 850 during World War I, so I was informed by other cattlemen.

I knew full well from conversations with the first Superintendent Hans M. Randolph, who had been there from 1908 to 1911, and from others that any administrative action adversely affecting grazing permits was extremely hazardous, very much like professional suicide. I conferred with one permit owner stating that I would terminate all cattle grazing within five years on Park lands and explained my reasons, that the number of head grazed would be reduced 20% each year and to plan accordingly. At that time I found him reluctant to sell range cattle, due to sharply declining prices then prevailing and thus lacked cash to pay for the annual permit already due. On July 1, 1921 he offered me and I accepted, in lieu of title to the 80 acre water tract owned by the permit dating. Subsequently, for the next ensuing three years I accepted in lieu of cash payments, progressive construction of a three strand barbed wire drift fence, using cedar posts, cut along the specified right of way, to permit any cattle in the future from grazing on Chapin mesa, where most of the ruins are which are visited by the public and within a maximum of 100 yards of the existing Park entrance road. Across the north rim where cattle were increasingly damaging both road surface when wet and bordering vegetative cover, the opportunity presented whereby emergency cooperation with Congressman Ed Taylor, meeting with his committee in Congress when this matter was brought to his attention, secured the final $5,000 needed to purchase the permit's final 320 acres of patented land; three wells on those lands were included and this completely terminated grazing in the Park.

During World War II, all of a sudden I got a wire from Senator Pat Mc-Carran, who represented the cattle interests, summoning me to a hearing he was conducting with his committee at Glenwood Springs, Colorado on petition of the Mancos cattlemens association opposing Park policy of non-grazing on the Mesa Verde. Congressman Robert Rockwell met me as I went in and said: "There are 200 cattlemen in there, Jess, and they're all agin' you and I wish you well." After I had given my history of the Park, McCarran got up and said, "I'm sorry gentlemen, but we must deny your request unless you prove there are no other Federal lands, or other lands suitable for grazing that you cannot get." And added, "I tell you very frankly you will have a most difficult task proving that fact." That ended the grazing. I drove McCarran to the Brown Palace in Denver after this hearing and had dinner with him that night with my ranger present. At one point the Senator kicked the ranger under the table and said to me, "Superintendent Nusbaum, I would like to obtain a permit to graze cattle in the Park." I answered, "Senator, you can come to the Park and graze cattle — ONE CALF — providing you keep it on a leash." He let out a whoop.

The Eighth National Park Service Conference — the first ever to be held in Mesa Verde — took place at Park Headquarters October 1-6, 1925. It was attended by many Park Superintendents and Park naturalists, some National Monument personnel, Director Mather, Assistant Director Horace M. Albright, Chief Engineer and Dr. L.I. Hewes the Deputy Commissioner, Bureau of Public Roads. The two most important subjects to be discussed were the expansion of educational work through the Park system and the development of good roads under the road budget in cooperation with the Bureau of Public Roads.

On the final day, at the request of Chief Engineer Burrell, I drove him over the high north rim section of the Park entrance road, running into a heavy shower just as I started down grade from the crest of Park Point, elevation 8575 feet. Burrell became greatly agitated when the car started to slip sideways toward the benched-in drainage ditch. He told me to apply the brakes, next to shift to lower gear. I told him this was futile as we purposely graded benched-in roadways so any car without chains would ditch itself due to any lack of gravel surfacing on such clay-shale roadways. We would wait a half hour or more then proceed as usual without chains. He insisted I put on chains at once.

When we got back to headquarters, he immediately conferred with Mather, Albright and Hewes saying it was imperative that Park roads be gravelled as soon as possible. He urgently recommended a $160,000 allotment of road funds for this project due to the long haul and excessive climb to the top of the Mesa, from the nearest Mancos Valley source. The following morning after more showers most of the Park personnel who attempted to leave without chains got ditched for an hour or two before they could return to Park Head-quarters for another day. Finally, about a year later, Mather wired me that $55,000 was being transferred for this project from Crater Lake National Park.

I was still feeling pretty low when Pete Reynolds, manager of the big smelter at Durango and a competent geologist, came to the Park for another weekend visit with me. I took him by car and hiking to the southeast tip of Chapin Mesa, on the Soda Canyon side, 900 feet above the Mancos River, where we sat on the rim with our feet dangling over the high vertical cliff wall. It was a bright warm day. Pointing out to Pete the location of the Two Story House, the first cliff dwelling photographed by W.H. Jackson in 1874, and then other points of interest. Suddenly I told Pete I thought from the feel that I had my hand on $55,000 worth of gravel.

Pete said, "What's the matter, Jess; is this heat getting you?"

I answered, "No, but I am reluctant to look."

Pete, looking surprised, answered, "Let's find a break in the rim rock to get down to where we can see what you are feeling with your hand." He did.

It was the same type of gravel found along the Mancos River, from its source in the high La Plata Mountains, to its entry into the head of Mancos Canyon through the Mesa Verde. This isolated remnant was a conglomerate mass of loose gravel embedded in a cement of hard clay, since it was deposited atop the Mesa Verde sandstone cap-rock by the Mancos River when it flowed over the Mesa millions of years before it created the 900 foot deep canyon at this point. I was reminded of Wallace W. Atwood's classic publication, THE ROCKY MOUNTAINS and what he said on pages 157-58: "Similar outwash silts and gravels of this basin filling, spread westward over the surface of the Colorado Plateau. Some of these gravels are now present on the surface of Mesa Verde, southwest of the San Juan Mountains, in Colorado and at an elevation of about 7,800 feet above sea level. The famed Mesa has been isolated by later erosion, but it was once a part of the widespread surface developed by erosion and filling just before the last great mountain making period of the West. Remnants of such gravel deposits have been discovered on peneplain surfaces of the San Juan Mountains, as high as 12,000 feet."

This tip of Chapin Mesa was on Ute Reservation land, about five miles south of the south boundary of Mesa Verde Park. Therefore, this gravel bar was the property of the Wiminuchi Band of Southern Utes. Since it was practically devoid of grazing resources and miles from the nearest source of water supply I thought the Ute Council, always seeking more funds from the Federal Government, would be eager to sell gravel to the Mesa Verde National Park.

Toward this objective, I first confered with Superintendent E.E. McKeen of the Consolidated Agency at Ignacio, since he was also in charge of the Sub-Agency at Towaoc which administered Wiminuchi Band affairs. Then, per his suggestion, I conferred with members of the Tribal Council best known to me. They were wholly opposed. McKeen then suggested that it would probably be necessary to "play Santy Claus, as others do." I probably expended in the neighborhood of $100 of personal funds in making gifts directly and through the Mancos Creek Trading Post, again to no purpose.

That Autumn, as for several years previously, at Director Mather's suggestion and the request of Congressman Louis C. Cramton, Chairman of the House Sub-Committee on Interior Department Appropriations, I accompanied and facilitated Committee hearings on justifications for estimated expenditure for the ensuing fiscal year for the Indian Service from Taos Pueblo, west of the Navajo and Ute Agencies in New Mexico and Mesa Verde National Park. This 1926 Sub-Committee then included Congressman Edward T. Taylor, Fred J. Bailey of the Bureau of the Budget, Charles Rhodes, Commissioner of the Office of Indian Affairs, Associate Commissioner Scattergood, and two other Congressmen. Enroute I explained to Mr. Cramton and his entourage the current status of the Mesa Verde gravel situation and the Ute Tribal impasse. Cramton sent work to McKeen to assemble the Ute Tribal Council and an interpreter at the Towaoc Sub-Agency for a hearing two days later.

The hearing which Cramton conducted was a notable one. Four of the five Council members, after reviewing past grievances against the Government since the Treaty of 1868, stated that I wanted to crush the gravel and secretly remove the gold and then put the residue on the Mesa Verde roads to fool them. Each ended with the common statement, "Nusbaum leave the gravel alone."

In an aside, Cramton told me the whole case was against Mesa Verde, that the Committee wanted to help me — he would call on me next and to make my presentation strong and clear. This I did to the Committee's satisfaction, relating the highlights of the pertinent data above reported.

Then Mr. Cramton called on "Buckskin Charlie," head of the Ute Tribal Council and hereditary Ute Chief. Again he reviewed all past grievances with the Government, then said firmly, "Nusbaum tell them nice story about how the Mancos River first flowed over the top of Mesa Verde and leave the gravel up there long long time, millions of years ago, and then cut the Mancos River Canyon 900 feet deep where it is now. That's a long long long time. When the Mancos Rivers fills up the canyon and again makes the gravel wet, that's soon enough to begin to talk. Meanwhile, Nusbaum, he leave the gravel alone."

Cramton then told them that the Government — the Congress which they represented made appropriations for the Utes for Mesa Verde, that it was Congress who wanted the gravel and would pay them for it, for use on mesa Verde roads — not Nusbaum who was only their agent in charge. He asked them to sell the gravel to Congress. Their answer was unitedly, "No."

Mr. Cramton spoke of cooperation with the Congress then he asked

McKeen when the next quarterly payment from the Ute Tribal Fund was due. McKeen answered that all members of the Wiminuchi Band, 643 on the current roll, were due to receive a $50 Fund payment on October 15th. He stated that the Autumn payment was the most important of all since they needed money to buy Winter clothing, shoes, blankets and other supplies. Cramton again reiterated that there was no truth to the story that the trader at Towaoc, Henry Crawford, spread, about gold in the gravel that Nusbaum wanted for himself and he would hold up the Autumn payment for further council.

Utes, expecting payment on October 15th began coming to Towaoc earlier. By October 15th the demands for payments became so strong that McKeen was called to Towaoc to further explain the delay. One of the heaviest snowfalls occurred a day or two later. Then Buckskin Charlie and the other members of the Tribal Council went to McKeen and stated that "Nusbaum could have all the gravel he wants at whatever price he wants to pay, but the Utes want their October 15th payment, now."

Superintendent McKeen asked them to sign a paper to this effect. They steadfastly refused to sign any papers, stating that the last time the Utes signed a paper, the Government took their Mesa Verde lands. Due to this impasse, he told them to go separately to five different persons, including himself, and tell each that they were willing to sell the gravel to Mesa Verde at whatever price the Government would pay, as each did. The Trust Fund payments were released and paid after this information was conveyed to Congressman Cramton and the Office of Indian Affairs. Cramton was so impressed with McKeen's abilities that he recommended to Mr. Rhodes that McKeen be promoted and transferred to the Superintendency of the Rosebud Reservation in South Dakota.

In 1939, Paul R. Franke, Sr., then Superintendent of Mesa Verde, was called upon by the U.S. General Accounting Office for a copy of the contract between Mesa Verde National Park and the Consolidated Ute Agency, under which Mesa Verde had purchased and paid approximately $4,500 for gravel over a period of years (over 90,000 cubic yards at 5¢ per yard). Franke couldn't locate a written document or contract and frantically appealed to me for help. I gave him pertinent history of the oral contract, why it was impossible to negotiate and written and signed contract, and told him of McKeen's statement that he was responsible and had all the facts if the question ever again came up in Washington. Our explanations cleared the lack of a written contract and payments made under oral contract.

Early in 1939, as I was motoring along the canyon rim road which I planned and constructed between Cliff Palace and Balcony House, so that visitors could see the many ruins in the canyon walls without entering them and enjoy the finest scenic command of Cliff and Soda Canyons enroute. Midway on the promontory of their junction, 900 feet above the canyon floor, a special overlook was provided which extended the view down Soda Canyon to the walls of main Mancos Canyon. When I stopped there, as I always did to enjoy the notable canyon scene, I was appalled to see an advancing bulldozer ripping up dense sagebrush, shrubbery and related forest cover along the drainage channel of Soda Canyon and irreparably scarring the canyon scene.

Since time was of the essence, I rushed back to headquarters, phoned Don Wattson, Superintendent of the Consolidated Ute Agency at Ignacio, and told him to stop forthwith any bulldozing of a road up Soda Canyon. He was very reluctant to do so, saying they planned to build some stock watering dams atop Moccasin Mesa and would be trucking cement and sand to the foot of Wild Horse Trail, then use pack horse transport to the tank locations. In response, I stated that I would phone Secretary of the Interior Harold Ickes. What that bulldozer was doing to Mesa Verde environment! Later that afternoon the bulldozer was no longer visible from the main road.

I suggested to Don Watson, Mesa Verde Park archaeologist, that he check up further with Wattson on the fact that the Indian Service was building a road in Mancos Canyon, due to implications to the scores of small ruins and some sizeable ones on the floor of the canyon. Watson reported to the Director, with copy to me, that many sites within staked right-of-way were severely damaged or destroyed and that a number of small sites well distant from right-of-way had also been excavated by bulldozer means.

Acting Director Demaray discussed this wholesale damaging and destruction with Commissioner John Collier of the Indian Service. He refuted Watson's statements stating that no Indian would damage or destroy archaeological sites. When Mr. Demaray so reported to Watson and me, Watson prepared and submitted to the Director and to me copies of a comprehensive, photographically illustrated report, of each site damaged or destroyed both within the right-of-way as well as distant therefrom. Photos of this latter group show the tracks of the dozers to and through the sites.

On the basis of the report, Commission Collier and Acting Director Demaray for the National Park Service drafted a Memorandum of Understanding, approved by Secretary Ickes of Interior on January 3, 1940, resulting in suitable warning signs being erected by the Office of Indian Affairs and teeth were put in the effort to apprehend and secure the conviction of pot hunters.

When, in September 1927, my road contractor failed his bonding company, they told me I must hire my help in Mancos and the town council of Cortez wanted people hired there also. It got so troublesome I phoned trader friends in Shiprock and through that area, and said, "Send me Navajos; I'll pay them cash for I have a job to do." The Navajos came up. Little bands together would take a contract for so many yards in a station, measured by the engineer for them. They would work 18 to 20 hours at a stretch using hand methods; and we were getting this job done for 15 to 20¢ per cubic yard what the steam shovel and contractor had failed to do at 75¢ per yard. From then on I had Navajos on the Park. I used them for all purposes. I could take them out on the road and they would care for themselves and live right there. They appreciated a little commissary and they always paid up. When they got their money they would tie it up in the corner of a little cotton sack, turn it over to me and if they wanted such items as saddles, I made the effort to get it wholesale. As a result I kept a place of safekeeping for their cash and looked after their orders to mutual satisfaction.

This cooperation with the Navajos was why, after the campfire talks over a period of 10 years, we could have Navajo programs in addition. Always six of the best Navajos were picked and put in authentic costume and they gave their songs, two parts of the Yeibichai (Navajo dances of the Gods) and one of their Circle dances. This always proved a highlight for visitors and the Navajo were superb. The ranger passed the hat for a small contribution and the leader got 25¢ more than the others, who got an equal share. After this was initiated, an agent from the accounting office in Washington came in to complain that no accounting was made of this. We replied that the Navajo would do this, but they insisted the ranger continue and we had to refuse. After that the Navajos did pass the hat themselves, they would carefully lay the money out on a rock at the campfire circle and they did their own dividing.

When Congress failed to provide funds requested for the first four-rooms of a fire-proof masonry wall unit for a Park Museum to house the collections then exhibited in an inflammable vault cabin, Mrs. Stella M. Levinson of San Francisco, who was concerned as a result of her visits in 1921 and 1922, gave me a check for $3,000, and later $2,000 more toward construction of the first unit.

In 1924, John D. Rockefeller, Jr. and his three older sons visited the Park with Dr. R.W. Corwin, his long-time friend from Pueblo, Colorado, I conducted them through the ruins for the better part of two days' time I could spare and on their final afternoon Rockefeller asked if I would take him over the headquarters area and outline for him a planning for future development. He asked why I had not completed the building which I said was the new museum, then at ceiling level and I explained lack of water during travel season: not enough to care for tourist needs and to mix mud for mortar, and that private funds for its completion had been exhausted. He replied, "Why private? This is a public thing that the Congress should do." I answered that Congress had rejected it. "Well," he answered, "This is one of those cases where it's usually up to some person of means to demonstrate the feasibility and merit of doing something which Congress is not interested in because they are too busy getting reelected, as that is their principal concern." He added, "I'll chip in, pledge now for funds to complete the building and buy the finest type exhibit cases we can get with bronze bands and plate glass." We made the cases. Also, at this same time he provided funds for the excavation of ruins to increase the collections and to enhance them. Later in 1926 he returned and gave us more for additional cases.

The Museum in total was practically built by friends of the Park with no solicitation, and our own back-breaking labor. Some nine years later when he was Administrator of the Public Works Program Secretary Harold L. Ickes secured some $22,500 which was used to improve this project, plus funds for drilling a desperately needed well.

If you think for a moment that the Colorado Senator had given up, you are sadly mistaken. In early 1923, he arranged a game of golf with President Harding and asked him to terminate me. Answer? "No soap." He then arrived at Secretary Work's office bearing two volumes of letters, all charging me with some form of mismanagement. He wanted Harold Work to fire me forthwith. Work knew me well and he asked the Senator, "If you will leave these with me I will review them, but I cannot do it now." As soon as the Senator had departed, he called the Park Service office in Washington and a conference with Assistant Director Cammerer was set up. When he arrived, Work said, "Lawrence, the Senator who has been after Jess has been here and wants me to discharge him; I know what it is. Here is the record of his charges — take these damned books down to the Park Service and lose them." He did, but I saw them. Once again in late 1925 the Senator repeated his request to President Coolidge at a White House reception and again he got no where. It took all that time, from 1920 through 1925, but it did sadden me for in his charges he had stated that among other things I paid no attention to ordinary people, only the wealthy and intellectual.

In the Spring of 1924, the Navajos completed the Knife Edge road on the old line. It cut the distance of the Park entrance road by four miles. A short time later two more short cuts took off two more miles, so the road was now but 12 miles — six miles shorter. We then made a morning and afternoon loop for tourists, bringing the trips to greater advantage regarding view, and as we had built sections of the loops right near the rim of the canyons, there was a command of scenery and scores of cliff dwellings that had not been viewed before. Looking at the ruins never deteriorates them, so it enhanced the entire attractiveness of the area and saved more of the archaeology.

In 1927, the Assistant Secretary of the Interior with the Director of the National Park Service came to consult with me. I had been sending in reports of violations of the Antiquities Act to them since 1921, which had taken place in the four corners region of Colorado, New Mexico, Arizona and Utah. They were with me for two days and Mr. Ickes finally said, "There's only one way this can be controlled: we must make Jess our field man and we will get Secretary Work to make the immediate appointment." Secretary Work did just that, naming me to the position of "Consulting Archaeologist for the Secretary of the Interior," taking place in mid-1927.

I now had authority in the field for conformity with the Antiquities Act, to report and take up any violation, and in emergency to act for the department. While I was serving in this position, the Secretary's office sent me more than 500 applications for scientific permits for museums and qualified places, submitting records of these until my retirement in 1958.

POT HUNTING

If you have an idea that the Wetherills were the first ones to discover the ruins of the Mesa Verde, don't believe that old myth. Father Silvestre Vélez Escalante left Santa Fe on the last day of July 1776, heading up a small expedition to blaze a trail from Santa Fe along and across the Colorado River canyon because it was the only way they could get through to California and the coastal missions, because there was concern of a Russian threat from the north.

Escalante named most of the rivers: the Animas, the Dolores, the Mancos and others along his route. He kept a marvelously good record. I have gone with Herbert E. Bolton (Historian; Professor, University of California, Berkeley) over a good part of that route. As we followed it Bolton would always say, "If where you're going doesn't match with what Escalante said, you are off the trail."

At Mancos, Colorado, Escalante kept to the foothills and the valleys. At the time he was suffering from chills and fever because he was susceptible to damp and cold, conditions he found there in August 1776. He remained at Mancos for two days and as the Mesa Verde is the most conspicuous mesa in the area for it commands everything, he did not mention it and passed it by.

By the time he got to the Dolores River he had recovered enough to begin once again to describe everything he saw, including the great big ruins there. Not being prepared for severe Winter, he had to give up after he got to Lake Utah, just south of Salt Lake City. He came southward through Zion, along the Virgin and got to the Colorado River...their food supply having given out, they were eating horse meat.

He made the first crossing of the Colorado River in its canyon depth at the place we now know as the "Crossing of the Fathers." I took Bolton to it and was unsuccessful in trying to get him across, so I had Norman Nevills take us both down the San Juan by boat to get there.

Others had been through the Mancos area, as had my great friend William Henry Jackson (famous photographer with the Hayden Survey), who went through Mancos canyon photographing for the first time the great cliff dwellings there. He had a guide, name of Captain John Moss (agent for Tibercio Parrot and the Parrot Brothers of San Francisco for whom Parrot City, a mining camp near Hesperus, Colorado, was named), who had paid the Utes $25,000 to placer mine the Hesperus River. He was representing others who had made fortunes placer mining the Sacramento River in California. He was friendly with the Utes, but Jackson nevertheless recounted when on the Hayden Survey on the San Juan they were constantly harassed by Utes. As a result in 1874, Jackson got through once again and in spite of Moss's friendship with them they still ran off his horses. Back in 1873, the artist of the Hayden Survey was there and I have sketches he made, 10 x 13 of Cliff Palace.

A prospector and coal miner working the canyons of the Mesa Verde, S.E. Osborn wrote of the ruins in a letter to the *Denver Republican*, boasting and urging the Government to protect both the Aztec ruins and those of Mesa Verde. Osborn came with two men named Hayes and Manuel in 1883 and stayed through 1884, the heaviest snowfall year in the history of that country. So deep was the snow that year that the D&RG Railway got through only once to Durango in 1884 in 77 days. South, where they finally broke through to get to Farmington, New Mexico, it was six feet deep.

There were others there and I have personally talked with an alert gentleman, Henry Morgan, then 93 years of age. He recounted for me that he moved into the valley in 1872 and was grazing cattle atop the Mesa Verde by 1875. Finally he said, "The Wetherills got through down there and with a few cattle and they were always in trouble and against me, their cattle wanted to follow mine as we brought them off the Mesa Verde." He added, "My partner and I built a cabin down Mancos canyon in 1874, so we could graze our cattle which we drove by oxen in the Winter." He went on, "One late evening in 1879, a swarthy little man riding a little brown stallion rode in and said, my name is B.K. Wetherill; I was a former Indian Agent in Pennsylvania; I want to build a home in that little grove of cottonwoods across the way. I'm scared of the Utes — I wonder if I could live with you?" Morgan took him in. He lived that way with Morgan for two years and finally built a log cabin in the cottonwoods, across the Mancos River in 1881.

RICHARD WETHERILL

The Wetherills didn't go into the canyon until 1887. They were the ones who explored most of the ruins. There was no law at that time to prevent taking and ravaging and looting of hundreds of Mesa Verde sites, which they did, and in consequence did a great deal of damage.

Richard Wetherill became field manager of all Hyde Exploration (Benjamin Talbot Babbitt and Frederick E. Hyde, Jr., auspices American Museum of National History: National Archives, Washington, D.C.) expedition activities. Richard made a homestead entry in 1896 for the Chaco Canyon lands in New Mexico, on which the great Pueblo Bonito and adjacent major pueblo ruins were located and soon inaugurated a major program of excavation within Pueblo Bonito, on the false assumption that the Expedition had acquired sole and exclusive excavation rights.

In early April 1900, Dr. Edgar L. Hewett, then collaborating with the General Land Office in Washington in securing protection for ruins and anti-quities on Federal lands owned or controlled by the Department of the Interior, complained of flagrant archaeological vandalism in Pueblo Bonito. Hewett had examined the 13 major Chaco Canyon pueblo ruins some years before (see: *The New Mexican*, April 30, May 1, 1900 and Archives Society, Santa Fe).

To counter Hewett's complaints, Richard Wetherill persuaded Special Agent Max Pracht of the Santa Fe Federal Land Office to defend the program of excavation, for which Dr. Frederick W. Putnam represented the American Museum of National History and advised as excavations progressed.

Ordered by a General Land Office letter dated December 18, 1900, Special Agent S.J. Holsinger of the Phoenix, Arizona office made a very com-prehensive and detailed report of all aspects of this whole Chaco Canyon ruin situation, submitting his related report December 5, 1901, requesting suspension of Richard Wetherill's homestead entry and any further excavations by the Hyde Exploring Expedition. The commissioner of the General Land Office formally ap-proved the Holsinger report and cancelled the Wetherill homestead entry and pro-hibited any further excavations by the Hyde Exploring Expeditions.

JOHN F. LACEY

Lacey, Representative from the State of Iowa, widely recognized as one of the greatest convervationists who ever sat in Congress, came to Santa Fe in the Summer of 1902 to accompany Edgar L. Hewett on a comprehensive survey of the heritage of Pueblo ruins of the Pajarito Plateau, and to observe the flagrant damaging, destruction and loss of archaeological values caused by un-scientific methods of pot hunters and commercial exploitation.

The Antiquities Act, written in collaboration with Hewett and approved on June 8, 1906, is actually a combination of two bills from the 1904 Congress. One, the Rodenburg Bill, placed aboriginal or archaeological ruins in the custody of the Secretary of the Interior with authority to control excavation and to prevent vandalism. The other was introduced by Lacey asking the President to establish Parks by proclamation. The word "parks" was changed to "monuments." The words "objects of historical and scientific interest,"— which are why the larger Na-tional Monuments are set up — were taken over by the National Park Bill.

The law stated that "Monuments should be limited to the smallest area compatible with the care and preservation of the objects to be protected." That sentence was placed in the Lacey Bill in order to get rid of a specific limitation in the Rodenburg Bill which dealt only with antiquities and confined them to 640 acres — one square mile. This provision served as a legal guide to the President in the exercise of his delegated powers.

Practically all of the Mesa Verde cliff dwellings and most of the lesser ruins were situated south of the north boundary of the Southern Ute Reservation. Under the Act of June 29, 1906, establishing Mesa Verde National Park, only Federal lands lying outside or north of this boundary could be embraced within the Park at that time due to the opposition of the Wiminuchi Utes and their Tribal Council to relinquish a single acre of their ceded lands.

To counter this opposition, the original proviso in Section 2 of the Act of June 29, 1906 was amended and placed all prehistoric ruins on Indian lands within 5 miles of all boundaries of the Park under the custodianship of the Secretary of the Interior, to be administered by the same service that is established for the Custodianship of the Park.

THE DINOSAUR SKELETONS

There is another story in this connection, Rosemary, that concerns a very large dinosaur's fossilized remains, exposed in the bank of Montezuma Creek along the southern part of the Colorado-Utah border. Dr. Barnum Brown, at that time the dinosaur authority for the American Museum of National History in New York City, ascertained that Earl Morris, the archaeologist, had made archaeological surveys up that drainage.

In 1908, Dr. Byron Cummings was making archaeological surveys in southeastern Utah and he asked A.V. Kidder, who was making his first visit, to accompany him on a survey of sites along that drainage. Travelling along the left hand branch of Montezuma Creek, they encountered a fully whiskered old man on horseback who asked them what they were doing up there in his cattle range. They answered that they were looking for archaeological sites and asked what he knew. He replied that he had seen some ruins up there but knew nothing about them and added, "but if you are looking for serpents, you will find some exposed in the north bank of the arroyo...there's the biggest Goddamned serpent I've ever seen — it's a quarter of a mile in length!"

Kidder had mailed to the American Museum thereafter for their interest the fact that they had found in the arroyo bank, in situ, the extremely large vertebrae of three separate dinosaurs. When Kidder wrote me about this a decade later, he asked if Barnum Brown had ever been issued the required permit by the Department of the Interior to make a survey. I was handling these matters and replied that he did have the required permit, but it had been issued in the early 1930s and that Brown, accompanied by Morris, had made a field examination, but nearly ten years before using the permit which he had held all this time. He, Brown, reported that by the time Morris arrived, floods had caved in the banks and widened the arroyo and as a result they found the formerly articulated dinosaur remains had been carried downstream for several miles by waters; that only a paucity of the former remains were found.

SALVAGE

Over the years I had made numerous appeals to Congressmen in my attempt to administer the Antiquities Act and it led to a most gratifying experience, shared not only by myself but many others who cooperated in the consuming effort in 1950. On two days' notice I found that a major industry, El Paso National Gas Company, was about to build a gas-pipeline from near the south border of Mesa Verde, the Colorado River, across the Navajo Reservation. (See: Nusbaum, Jesse. *Pipeline Archaeology*. "Reports of Salvage Operations in the Southwest: El Paso National Gas Company Projects, 1950-1953." Laboratory of Anthropology and Museum of Northern Arizona: 1956.) I made a prompt study and took the matter up with the officials of the company, telling them they would violate the Antiquities Act and destroy scores of the important archaeological sites in the right-of-way, no matter what route they took over the Navajo and Hopi Reservations and also on the Flagstaff National Forest.

I had authority from the Secretary to act in such cases, and in consultation, suggested they avoid cost of penalties by following my recommendations, by agreeing to pay the cost of scientifically salvaging, in accordance with the Antiquities Act, the archaeological sites and ruins they would otherwise destroy. They agreed to put this in effect within 24 hours, providing I would recruit the archaeologists, manage and supervise the project.

I agreed.

They provided a jeep and four-wheel drive station wagon for each team of two archaeologists. They would, and did, fly me wherever I was needed and we started. Rosemary turned a large room in our home into a bachelors quarters with three beds, making it possible for the young archaeologists on the teams working on salvage to make weekend reports to me. She cooked for them, washed for them if needed, typed and generally lightened the load I carried, for I had my regular assignment to carry out for the National Park Service. She rendered a final yeoman's service by cataloguing much of this early salvage material, where it can now be seen and studied by scholars in the extensive sherd-library at the Laboratory of Anthropology in Santa Fe.

In the ten years ensuing, other companies did the same thing. In more than 7,000 miles of pipe line right-of-way, 40 to 50 feet wide, we used 39 archaeologists and salvaged the value of 1,315 sites which would have been dstroyed. The area covered ran from El Paso, Texas, to Summas on the Canadian border; across New Mexico, Arizona and Utah. The nearest approach was when we came in on the Colorado Interstate's pipeline from Rock Springs, Wyoming to just outside Denver; and we found material coming past Greeley, Colorado, my birthplace, to near Fort Bent outside Denver, and lots of it in Wyoming.

Most of these 39 young men got their doctorates later. They made good salaries, for avoiding delay for the companys saved them large sums. This same principal of salvage which I devised, was to have the fellows walk the line in front of the bulldozers and observe and save every surface value before a dozer came up to destroy them. Then they dropped back and followed the trencher, which cut a wide trench up to five or six feet deep in which to lay the pipe, and thus would reveal in pipe line walls — in profile — the sites where nothing had been left on the top which they had first observed and covered.

We got a good number of subterranean sites in this way. That same principal was applied next to highways, first in New Mexico, where I cooperated with the engineers of the Bureau of Public Roads and with the State Highway Engineer. This policy has been extended nationwide and is now used on all of the roads under the super-system of National highways.

IMPORTANT EVENTS IN THE
PREHISTORY AND HISTORY OF MESA VERDE

1000 B.C. Occupancy of the Cliff Palace cave by first agricultural Indians of the Southwest. Date represents archaeologist's approximation of the earliest known use of the caves of Mesa Verde by man.

500 B.C. Estimated date of the second agricultural people. Their habitations extended over the entire Mesa Verde and their culture excelled in the introduction and perfection of many arts.

1073 A.D. Cliff Dweller civilization. Construction of Cliff Palace.

1776 Expedition of Padre Silvestre Velez de Escalante to Southwestern Colorado. Party camped at the base of the Mesa Verde.

1859 Ascent of the north escarpment of Mesa Verde by Captain J.N. Macomb of the U.S. Army and members of his party of geologists.

1874 Discovery of the ruins in the Mancos Canyon by W.H. Jackson of the U.S. Geological Survey. Party attacked by Ute Indians.

1888 Discovery of Cliff Palace and other ruins by Alfred and Richard Wetherill.

1891 First organized archaeological expedition to Mesa Verde under direction of Baron G. Nordenskiöld. Collection of valuable archaeological data and important scientific publication "The Cliff Dwellers of the Mesa Verde."

1906 Mesa Verde National Park created June 29.

1907 Excavation Spruce Tree House by Dr. J. Walter Fewkes of the Smithsonian Institution.

1908 Hans M. Randolph appointed first superintendent of Mesa Verde. Excavation of Cliff Palace.

1910 Excavation of Cliff Palace completed. First six miles of road on top of mesa from Spruce Tree Camp to north rim constructed.

1910 Excavation and repair of Balcony House by J.L. Nusbaum. S.E. Shoemaker appointed superintendent.

1913 Entrance road completed. First automobile in Spruce Tree Camp. Thomas Rickner appointed superintendent. Extension of park boundaries to include valuable ruins and archaeological remains.

1914   Construction of the Prater and Morfield Canyons road and first wagon road to ruins.

1915   Sun Temple excavated by Dr. Fewkes.

1916   National Park Service Act passed August 25, Far View House excavated by Dr. Fewkes.

1917   First government-constructed trails to Spring House and Soda Canyon. Stephen T. Mather made first Director of National Park Service.

1918   First hotel service at Spruce Tree Camp. Inauguration of museum exhibits.
1919   Square Tower House excavated.

1921.   Establishment of superintendent's office and home at Spruce Tree Camp. Jesse L. Nusbaum appointed superintendent.

1925   Park museum constructed from donated funds and opened to public.

1926   Excavation of Step House Ruin and discovery of early occupation of cave by Basket Maker III culture pre-dating the Cliff Dwellers by 1000 years or more.

1928   Exclusive jurisdiction of park tendered to the United States and accepted by Act of Congress April 25.

1931   New entrance highway completed and surfaced. Visitors: 18, 003, the largest number in park history.

BIBLIOGRAPHY

BEALE, E.F. "Wagon Road from Fort Defiance to the Colorado River." House Exec. Doc. No. 124, 35th Congress, 1st Session, Washington, D.C., 1858.

BIRDSALL, WILLIAM RANDALL. 'The Cliff Dwellings of the Cañons of the Mesa Verde." *American Geographical Society Bulletin*, Vol.XXIII, No.4, Part 1, December 31, 1891.

BLANCHE, JACQUES-EMILE. *Portraits of a Lifetime: The Edwardian Pagent, 1870-1914.* New York: Coward McCann, Inc., 1938.

CHURCHILL, ALLEN. *The Improper Bohemians.* New York: Ace Books, Inc., n.d.

DAVIS, W.W.H. *El Gringo or New Mexico & Her People.* Santa Fe: Rydal Press, 1938.

DRIGGS, HOWARD R. *Westward America.* New York: G.P. Putnam & Sons, 1942.

FRYXELL, FRITOF. "William H. Jackson: Pioneer, Photographer, Artist and Explorer." *The American Annual of Photography,* 1939.

GILLMOR, FRANCES, and WETHERILL, LOUISA WADE. *Traders to the Navajos.* Boston: Houghton Mifflin Co., 1934. Reprinted, Albuquerque: University of New Mexico Press, 1953.

GREGG, JOSIAH. "The Santa Fe Trade." *Diary & Letters of Josiah Gregg, 1840-1847.* Reprinted, Norman: University of Oklahoma Press, 1941.

HEWETT, EDGAR L. "Reports, Numbers 1 through 15." Archaeological Institute of America. Papers of the School of American Archaeology, Santa Fe: 1910-1913.

HOLMES, W.H. "Report on the Ancient Ruins of Southwestern Colorado, examined during the summers of 1875 and 1876." United States Geological and Geographical Survey of the Territories. Tenth Annual Report, Washington, D.C., 1901.

JACKSON, WILLIAM HENRY. "Ancient Ruins in Southwestern Colorado." United States Geological and Geographical Survey of the Territories for 1874. Eighth Annual Report. Washington, D.C., 1876.

_____. "Report on the Ancient Ruins Examined in 1875 and 1877." United States Geological and Geographical Survey of the Territories for 1876. Tenth Annual Report. Washington, D.C., 1878.

MACOMB, J.N. "From Santa Fe, New Mexico to the Great Colorado of the West." Report of the Engineering Department of the United States Army, Chapter 11. Washington, D.C., 1876.

MASON, CHARLES C. "The Story of the Discovery and Early Exploration of the Cliff Houses at the Mesa Verde." Denver: State Historical Society of Colorado, Unpublished Manuscript, 1917. Contains the notation that Richard Wetherill was "killed by the Navajos at Pueblo Bonito, New Mexico, June 22, 1910."

NEW MEXICO TERRITORIAL LEGISLATURE. "An Act to Establish a Museum for The Territory of New Mexico." Amended House Bill 100. New Mexico State Archives, Santa Fe, 1916.

NORDENSKIÖLD, GUSTAF A.E. Translated by D. Lloyd Morgan. *The Cliff Dwellers of Mesa Verde, Southwestern Colorado.* Stockholm: P.A. Norstedt & Söner, 1893.

NUSBAUM, JESSE L. "A Basket Maker Cave in Kane County, Utah." Monograph of the Museum of the American Indian. With notes on the artifacts by A.V. Kidder and J.S. Guernsey. New York: Heye Foundation, 1922.

_____. "Conservation of Antiquities on Public Domain." Report to the Southwest Division of the American Association for the Advancement of Science, El Paso: May 1, 1951.

_____. "Journals: 1907-1975." Unpublished Manuscripts, Santa Fe.

_____. "The New Laboratory of Anthropology at Santa Fe." *American Civic Annual*, Vol. III, 1931.

_____. "The New Museum of Art in Santa Fe." *Art & Archaeology*, Vol. VII, Archaeological Institute of America, 1919.

_____."The 1926 Reexcavation of Step House Cave, Mesa Verde National Park, Colorado." Monograph for the National Park Service, United States Department of the Interior, Mesa Verde: 1949.

_____. "Photography of Mesa Verde and Tributary Cañons: 1907-1908." Compiled with text notes by A.V. Kidder for the Report of Edgar Hewett to the Congressional Committee on the Preservation of American Antiquities.

_____. "Pipeline Archaeology, 1950-1953: The El Paso Natural Gas Projects." Laboratory of Anthropology, Museum of New Mexico, Santa Fe and Museum of Northern Arizona, Flagstaff, n.d.

_____. "Superintendents Monthly Reports: July 1921 through January 1930." National Park Service, United States Department of the Interior, Mesa Verde.

_____. "Tapes" of reminiscences as told to Rosemary Nusbaum.

NUSBAUM, JESSE L., and JOHNSON, TEMPLETON W. "Mission Churches in Rio Arriba, Santa Fe, Valencia, Bernalillo, Sandoval, McKinley, San Miguel, Guadalupe and Taos Counties. Reconnaissance Studies for the Art Museum in Santa Fe." *El Palacio*, Vol IV, No. 1. Santa Fe: Museum of New Mexico, 1916.

NUSBAUM, JESSE L. and MORLEY, SYLVANUS GRISWOLD. "Reconnaissance in Latin America: 1910-1913." Reports of the Museum of New Mexico. Santa Fe: 1910, 1911, 1912, 1913.

NUSBAUM, ROSEMARY. *The City Different and The Palace*. Santa Fe: The Sunstone Press, 1978.

RUDISILL, RICHARD. *Photographers of New Mexico Territory: 1854-1912*. Santa Fe: Museum of New Mexico Press: 1973.

SIMPSON, JAMES H. "Journal of a Military Reconnaissance from Fort Smith, Arkansas to Santa Fe, New Mexico." Reports of the Secretary of War. Sen. Exec. Doc. 12, 31st Congress, 1st Session, Washington, D.C., 1850.

_____. "Journal of a Military Reconnaissance from Santa Fe, New Mexico to the Navajo Country." Reports of the Secretary of War. Sen. Exec. Doc. 64, 31st Congress, 1st Session, Washington, D.C., 1850.

SPRINGER, FRANK. "Address" in dedication of the new Art Museum in Santa Fe, New Mexico, November 25, 1917. Reprinted in the Santa Fe *New Mexican*, Monday, November 26, 1917.

STALLINGS, W.S., Jr. "A Basket Maker II Date from Cave du Pont, Kane County, Utah." *Tree Ring Bulletin*, Vol 8, No. 1, July 1941.

UNITED STATES CONGRESS. "An Act for the Preservation of American Antiquities." 59th Congress, 1st Session, June 8, 1906. United States Congressional Record, Vol. XL. Reprints and explanation may also be found in the *Journal of American*

Archaeology, Vol. XI.

_____. "An Act to Establish the Mesa Verde as a National Park." 59th Congress, 1st Session, June 29, 1906. United States Congressional Record, Vol. XL, Part 9, page 8818.

WALTER, PAUL A.F. "The Cities That Died of Fear: The Story of the Saline Pueblos." Archaeological Institute of America. Papers of the School of American Archaeology, No. 35, Santa Fe: 1916.

_____. "Santa Fe County, New Mexico." Publication for the Santa Fe Board of Trade. Santa Fe: The New Mexico Printing Co., 1909.

WETHERILL, RICHARD. Letters, April 7, 1890 - March 21, 1902, to B.T.B. Hyde, F.E. Hyde, Jr., and George H. Pepper, in connection with the work of the Hyde Exploring Expedition. American Museum of Natural History, New York.

ABOUT THE AUTHOR

Rosemary L. Nusbaum was born and grew up in Marquette, Michigan. In 1929 she was awarded an R.N. degree from University Hospital, Chicago, Illinois. She moved to Santa Fe, New Mexico in 1932 and during World War II she worked as a Medical Pathologist for the U.S. Army Eighth Corps Area, stationed at Bruns General Hospital, Santa Fe.

She has a long and rich involvement in the arts and in addition to her literary skills she has studied sculpture with Eugenie Shonnard and ceramics with Warren Gilbertson in Santa Fe.

Her short stories and verse have appeared in numerous magazines and anthologies including the *Santa Fean, New Mexico Magazine, Southwest Lore in Poetry, Songs of the Free* and *Songwriters and Poets of America.*

Of her many honors and awards, she holds in great esteem her place as a member of "Composers, Authors and Artists of America," and the Sophrosyne Award, presented to her by the St. John's College Class of 1969 as the person that class felt to be the most "understanding."

Her first full-length book, *The City Different and The Palace,* the story of the Palace of the Governors and its role in Santa Fe history, was published in 1978 by The Sunstone Press, Santa Fe, New Mexico.

www.ingramcontent.com/pod-product-compliance
Lightning Source LLC
LaVergne TN
LVHW091224080426
835509LV00009B/1152